DISCOVERING WESTCAVE

Kathie and Ed Cox Jr. Books on Conservation Leadership

SPONSORED BY

THE MEADOWS CENTER
FOR WATER AND THE ENVIRONMENT
TEXAS STATE UNIVERSITY

Andrew Sansom, General Editor

Westcave grotto, looking toward the overhang. Photo by Jim Nix

DISCOVERING WESTCAVE

The Natural & Human History
of a Hill Country Nature Preserve

S. Christopher Caran & Elaine Davenport

Foreword by Andrew Sansom

TEXAS A&M UNIVERSITY PRESS : COLLEGE STATION

This paper meets the requirements
of ANSI/NISO Z39.48–1992 (Permanence of Paper).
Binding materials have been chosen for durability.
Manufactured in China by Everbest Printing through
FCI Print Group

LIBRARY OF CONGRESS CATALOGING-IN-PUBLICATION DATA

Names: Caran, S. Christopher, author. | Davenport, Elaine, 1946– author.
Title: Discovering Westcave : the natural and human history of a Hill Country
   nature preserve / S. Christopher Caran and Elaine Davenport.
Other titles: Kathie and Ed Cox Jr. books on conservation leadership.
Description: First edition. | College Station : Texas A&M University Press,
   [2016] | Series: Kathie and Ed Cox Jr. books on conservation leadership |
   Includes bibliographical references and index.
Identifiers: LCCN 2016010473| ISBN 9781623494599 (flexbound : alk. paper) |
   ISBN 9781623494605 (ebook)
Subjects: LCSH: Westcave Preserve (Tex.)—Guidebooks. | Natural
   areas—Texas—Travis County—Guidebooks. | Natural areas—Texas—Texas
   Hill Country—Guidebooks. | Westcave Outdoor Discovery Center—History. |
   Wildlife conservation—Study and teaching—Texas.
Classification: LCC QH76.5.T4 C37 2016 | DDC 333.7209764/31—dc23 LC record available
at https://lccn.loc.gov/2016010473

A list of other titles in this series is available at the end of the book.

We dedicate
this book to
JOHN F. AHRNS,
the Law West of the Pedernales,
Westcave Preserve Manager 1974–2010,
a nature genius &
everybody's best friend.

We thank you.
The neighborhood thanks you.
The Earth thanks you.

Buck and doe White-tailed Deer (*Odocoileus virginianus*) on alert. Illustration by Nancy McGowan

CONTENTS

FOREWORD

The Texas Hill Country is changing...and fast. The population of the region, beloved by all Texans, increased from around 800,000 in 1950 to 2,600,000 in 2000 and is expected to double again by 2030. This explosive growth has brought unprecedented stress on one of the most iconic geographies in the United States and threatens to destroy many of its most sensational natural features, most alarmingly, its lovely water features and springs. These remarkable sites have always been in danger of being loved to death, and there is no more illustrative metaphor for that vulnerability than the beautiful Hill Country grotto known as Westcave. Situated very close to the Pedernales River outside of Austin, the spectacular limestone grotto presented an irresistible temptation to trespassers, who very nearly destroyed it.

Enter a remarkable student of architect Frank Lloyd Wright, John Covert Watson, who owned for many years the property upon which the grotto is located. Watson, who treasured the beauty of his land and its natural significance, chased away hundreds of intruders through the years, most of whom did not share his desire to protect it. John Watson managed Westcave from a unique partnership with the Lower Colorado River Authority, which enabled an expansion of the preserve. In 1976 he recruited John Ahrns, who moved onsite with his family. From their double wide mobile home he began hauling out of the canyon more than 100 full-size garbage bags of trash that had been left by trespassers for decades. John Ahrns served as the sole preserve director and lead educator at Westcave for many years and created the respected environmental education program that now reaches more than 6,000 children each year.

During his tenure, Ahrns, who passed away in 2014, oversaw the construction of the Warren Skaaren Environmental Learning Center, which opened to the public on the vernal equinox, March 22, 2003. The building is a model of sustainable design and includes such features as ground-source heating and cooling, a solar energy panel, and a rainwater harvesting system. Project architect Robert Jackson's remarkable work was recognized with a 2003 Merit Design Award from the Austin Chapter of the American Institute of Architects. Skaaren, an environmental activist, was also a successful film producer whose works included *The Texas Chainsaw Massacre* and *Batman*.

Today, the Westcave Outdoor Discovery Center, thanks to the leadership of many dedicated donors and its capable executive director Molly Stevens, is a national leader in the Children and Nature Network. As the authors of this first guide to Westcave, Elaine Davenport and Chris Caran aptly illustrate that it is a beacon of hope in an all too beautiful but threatened region. I have been privileged to serve on its board of directors and am particularly grateful to REI for making the publication of their work possible.

Only by visiting and experiencing such wonders of nature will our children be inspired to dedicate themselves to making sure it will still be there for theirs.

—Andrew Sansom
General Editor, Kathie and Ed Cox Jr. Books on Conservation Leadership

PREFACE

The twentieth century saw the flowering of the conservation movement in the United States as hundreds of millions of acres were acquired and protected for their natural resource and outdoor recreation value. Today, even as we continue to acquire and protect outdoor spaces, we are seeing a significant shift away from outdoor play, recreation, and learning as children become more urbanized and tethered to technology and the indoor environment. The result is that many young adults have a tenuous connection to the natural world.

There are many vital reasons to advocate for children in nature, but perhaps the most urgent is to safeguard the conservation victories that have been hard-won over the last century by ensuring that our children develop strong ties to the outdoors.

Fewer children today have access to nature, adult mentors, and the inspiring experiences that accompany outdoor play and learning. One of the most significant challenges is the allure of technology. During the past two decades, childhood has moved indoors. With the average American boy or girl spending more than eight hours a day in front of electronic screens, there is an increasing divide between children and nature. That divide is linked to some of our most disturbing childhood trends, such as the rise in obesity, attention disorders, and depression. The good news? Research shows that kids who spend even a little bit of their day outside are healthier and happier and perform better academically.

At Westcave Outdoor Discovery Center we are deliberately moving against the tide. Our mission is to inspire people to develop a lifelong practice of protecting and enjoying nature, and the work we do is about conserving, educating, and collaborating.

Conserving: With seventy-six acres of precious Texas Hill Country, including our remarkable canyon and grotto, our effort to restore and protect this environment for our resident wildlife as well as our preserve visitors is our first responsibility. One spring and summer resident, the endangered Golden-cheeked Warbler, nests here regularly.

Educating: A growing number of visitors——currently more than ten thousand per year——come to Westcave Preserve, many with their school classmates, to learn about the preserve's unique geology and hydrology and its diverse flora and fauna. On weekends our four daily guided tours and nighttime star parties regularly fill up with families and adult visitors. During the summer we support El Ranchito—the overnight, nature immersion camp that has introduced the wonder and joy of the Texas Hill Country to hundreds of children from economically challenged communities.

Collaborating: The Children in Nature Collaborative of Austin catalyzes more than thirty member nonprofits from the area to work toward common goals related to reconnecting kids with nature. Westcave has stepped up to lead this collaborative because we know that when we form strategic alliances and share ideas and resources, our impact is greater.

Westcave offers all of the benefits that come from outdoor play and learning, helping our children become the next generation of environmental stewards. As they come to love nature, they will come to protect what they love: our precious resources and the natural beauty that we all need to thrive and survive.

Enjoy this guidebook to Westcave Outdoor Discovery Center and to our extraordinary history of place, purpose, and people.

—Molly Stevens
Westcave CEO and executive director

ACKNOWLEDGMENTS

As this list of acknowledgments grew ever longer, we realized that we were thanking not only those who helped with this book, but also those who have nurtured the Westcave Outdoor Discovery Center over its forty-year history. This list includes many expert and generous people and organizations. Without all of them, we would not have had the opportunity to write this book.

The most profound tip of the hat goes to John Covert Watson, without whom Westcave Outdoor Discovery Center would not exist. In 1974 this visionary conservationist purchased the twenty-five acres containing his favorite grotto with money willed to him by his Aunt Marjorie Watson, and the rest is history. No expression of thanks will ever be enough.

An equal round of thanks goes to the late John Ahrns (1947–2014), the resident manager and guardian par excellence of the preserve from 1974 to 2010, whose fond dream was to have a book such as this in print. Living on the land gave John the opportunity to make an extraordinary impact on Westcave Preserve. He also spent hours in the Austin History Center researching the area, interviewed neighbors about their family stories, and did relentless research on the science behind the preserve's remarkable ecology. He began and kept up to date many of the species listed in the appendixes. We are walking in your footsteps, John. His widow Brenda and their daughter Amber Ahrns Gosselin and son Jeff Ahrns were invaluable in filling in the history of their years living at the preserve.

We also offer undying gratitude to Lee Walker, who first visited the preserve in 1978 and who has remained the staunchest of allies ever since in so many ways. Lee Walker, John Watson, and John Ahrns are considered the triumvirate of Westcave's founding fathers. John Ahrns died in 2014, but John Watson and Lee Walker are still active supporters and were extremely generous with their time as we explored the preserve's forty-year history.

We also acknowledge Westcave's many long-term friends, unnamed here or elsewhere in the book, who have helped make Westcave a crown jewel. Those who have served on the board of directors or the preserve council and/or have been staff or volunteers have our humble thanks for the lasting impact they have made. Because of their good work we can be certain that future generations will sustain and enhance this Hill Country gem and the environmental education and conservation programs that flow from it.

Westcave's staff gave pivotal help, especially Amber Ahrns Gosselin (walking in her father's footsteps as Westcave's land manager) and Linda Wofford, associate director, who has been actively involved with Westcave since 1994. Linda and Amber enthusiastically contributed drafts on the subjects within their areas of expertise, read and commented on the entire manuscript, and offered substantive guidance throughout the process. Addie Broussard, administrative coordinator and natural science educator, served as the book's photo editor. Erich Rose, weekend preserve manager and natural science educator, also contributed drafts and comments. Others highly involved include Traci Ibarra, Jane Jones, Julia Mechler, Ryan Spencer, and Paul Vickery. We give a big thank you, of course, to Executive Director Molly Stevens, who provided superb guidance and coordination as well as the prefatory welcome message. In the "mega-friend of Westcave" category is Terri Siegenthaler, ranch steward of the nearby Shield Ranch, whose comments on the manuscript were invaluable.

The highest praise goes to list wrangler Nan Hampton, who not only observed and added species to the plants, list in appendix B but also checked *every* species in all the lists against the Integrated Taxonomic Information System (ITIS), the United States Department of Agriculture Natural Resources Conservation Service PLANTS Database, or the American Ornothological Union's *Checklist of North and Middle American Birds.*

Speaking of which, a big thank you goes to the experts who contributed to and/or reviewed the plants list. They include John Ahrns, Michael Brewster, Margaret Campbell, Bill Carr, John Chenoweth, Yvonne Baron Estes, Paul Fushille, John Gee, John Gerhart, Amber Ahrns Gosselin, Nan Hampton, Laura Hansen, Bob Harms, Kirsti Harms, Sirpa Harms, Marshall C. Johnston, David Lemke, Terri Siegenthaler, and Murray Walton. Taking care of the bird list were John Ahrns, Victor Emanuel, Ed Faire, Paul Fushille, John Gee, Jane Jones, Ethel Kutac, and Ron Martin. We are indebted to Dan Hardy for preparing the original version of the sidebar on butterflies, to Traci Ibarra and Erich Rose for contributing to the butterfly list, and to Robert Fulginiti for preparing the list of mosses. The list of amphibians and reptiles started by John Ahrns and David Bennett has stood the test of time. For the fish list we thank John Ahrns and Steven Hubbell as well as unnamed investigators with the Lower Colorado River Authority (LCRA) and Texas Parks and Wildlife Department. For the mammals list we relied on John Ahrns, David Bennett, Melissa Meierhofer, and Leah M. Miller, and for the invertebrates list, on Traci Ibarra, Erich Rose, and William H. Russell, as well as unnamed investigators with the LCRA and the Texas Speleological Survey.

We thank Dan Chapman for insight (and some quotes) about his longtime friend John Ahrns. Many of Westcave Preserve's neighbors or former neighbors helped with research on the area's modern history: Randy Barton, Don Casey, Ralph Combest, Loretta and Vernon Cook, Shirley and Leonard Fehrle, Leonard Fehrle Jr., Elnora Neumann Kneese, John McLaurin, Carol Sue Eberling Purcell, Murray and Felixa Walton, Camilla Wenmohs, and Bobby Wilson. Coy Lay Jr. and Gretchen Randolph, the grandchildren of Chester F. Lay, who owned the Westcave property from 1937 to 1966, enthusiastically offered historical details and family photos that informed almost thirty years of the preserve's human history.

The images in this book are a mixture of striking photos and original illustrations by gifted image makers. We are thrilled that Nancy McGowan, an exceptional artist and illustrator, has favored us with her remarkably lucid drawings of flora and fauna. Thanks also to photographers Bob Ball, Addie Louise Broussard, Amber Ahrns Gosseling, Greg Hursley, Traci Ibarra, Chris Keller, Heather Kuhlken, Melody Lytle, Arman Moreno, Michael A. Murphy, Jim Nix, Erich Rose, Nancy Scanlan, Steven Schwartzman, Cameron Spencer, Ron Sprouse, Molly Stevens, Paul Vickery, and Blaine T. Williams. Other photos were obtained courtesy of the Austin History Center, Texas General Land Office, and United States Geological Survey. Tim Hayes, Joel Lardon, and Drew Patterson provided graphic design and/or images for the outdoor environmental education panels at the Environmental Learning Center, some of which are reproduced in this book.

Linda Wofford's many skills include graphic design, which she contributed with grace and good humor. Our gifted mapmakers were J. Robert Anderson, Zixu Qiao, and Ryan Spencer. Brian Maebius favored us with his painting of a Yucca Moth. Additional original artwork came from Rene Braud and Nan Hampton. The Estate of Walter and William Staehely authorized reproduction of a nineteenth-century painting by Hermann Lungkwitz. We especially thank Ric Sternberg for his video work during the research for this book and on many previous Westcave projects. We relied on Robert Jackson, the architect responsible for the exquisite Warren Skaaren Environmental Learning Center (ELC), to guide us on the correct celestial path regarding the building's attributes. And we all thank Dan Lester of the Astronomy Department at the University of Texas at Austin for his original analemma calculations for the building's amazing solar observatory. There were legions of "trespassers" who played at the Westcave grotto in the 1960s and '70s, but we especially thank Marcia Ball, Yvonne Baron Estes, and Bill Brooks for sharing their detailed accounts.

We are happy to thank Samuel D. McCulloch, who helped with the chapter on history and prehistory, and Robert W. Baumgardner Jr., who reviewed parts of the text and associated figures and tables for both the geology and surface water and groundwater chapters. Thanks to Joe Freeman for his expertise regarding the Historic Homestead at Westcave Preserve and to Daniel J. Prikryl, Charles A. Hixson, and Andrew F. Malof for their work on the March 2013 Cultural Resources Survey by the LCRA. Thanks to Georgean and Paul Kyle, founders of Chaetura Canyon Sanctuary, part of Travis Audubon Society, for information on the Chimney Swift Tower at the preserve, which they donated and built. Thanks to Bob Rose, Linda Wofford, and Steven Hubbell for their original text for the Westcave brochures on the Solar Observatory, Nature's Numbers, and the Water Cycle.

We had expert guidance from Shannon Davies, our editor at Texas A&M University Press, who has a keen eye for a high-quality image and phrase and admirable experience in all things publishing. We feel lucky that Noel Parsons was assigned as our copy editor and Sue Gaines as our indexer. Both used their knowledge and skill with words to improve this project. Thanks also to the book's series sponsor, the Meadows Center for Water and the Environment at Texas State University and its visionary leader, Andrew Sansom.

Most of those named above, plus ourselves, would not have had the chance to make a difference at Westcave if it had not been for the individuals and organizations who were willing to marry their passion for a healthy environment with their generous offering of financial support for Westcave's outdoor conservation and education programs. At the top of this list are the Betty Norsworthy Family, the Brown Foundation, Buddy A. Davidson Foundation, Cynthia and George Mitchell Foundation, Educational Foundation of America, the Georgia B. Lucas Foundation Fund of the Austin Community Foundation, H-E-B, Hershey Foundation, Houston Endowment, Impact Austin, Jordan Family Foundation, Junior League of Austin, Michael Luigs, the Meadows Foundation, the Reese family, the Shield Ayres Foundation, Texas Parks and Wildlife Department, the Vickers-Walker family, the Warren Skaaren Trust, and the Winkler family.

We thank the many unnamed staff members of the Lower Colorado River Authority (LCRA), which bought Westcave Preserve in 1983 and expanded its boundaries in 2010, for their sustaining support over the years. Thanks also to the LCRA, the Warren Skaaren Trust, Texas Parks and Wildlife Department, and fundraising consultant Kirsten Ingram for their vision and collaboration to fund and build the Warren Skaaren Environmental Learning Center. The 2008 acquisition and funding of the Uplands, a parcel that more than doubled Westcave Preserve's footprint, was made possible by Board Chair Max Scoular together with Lee Walker and the major support of AMD Corporation, the Damuth Foundation, Chris Harte, the LCRA, and Pam and Mike Reese.

Thank you, Capital Area Master Naturalists, for nurturing one of the authors (Class of 2011 is the best!). And thanks always to our spouses, Blaine T. Williams and Kay Caran, for their support and understanding as we labored in the word mines—and to Blaine, especially, for his perceptive reading of the manuscript and his humorous takes on its particularly dense passages, which have been improved, we trust.

We humbly thank all of you, including others not named, who have contributed to our understanding of the subjects covered. All errors are, of course, our own. Undoubtedly, we have overlooked someone, and we apologize in advance.

Purple Cliffbrake (*Pellaea atropurpurea*) in summer.
Illustration by Nancy McGowan

ABOUT THE GUIDEBOOK

This guidebook is intended to introduce visitors to the natural and human history of Westcave, including its forty-year record of conservation and environmental education. In one volume the guide covers climate, geology, soils, animals, plants, water, ecology, archeology, history, and the role of Westcave in environmental education and preserving the environment, one sunrise at a time.

In this guidebook we list both the scientific and standard common names of all species known or likely to occupy the preserve. The names used and their spellings are those accepted at the time the guidebook was compiled. We have chosen to capitalize common names, although not all authorities take this approach. All common names in the text match common and scientific names in the species lists at the back of the book and in the index. Some of the names may be unfamiliar, but they are the key both to identifying a species and to obtaining more information about it. We hope the reader will draw from this guidebook the inspiration to seek experience and knowledge in the natural world.

This guide seeks to untangle the complex links between the ancient and the modern, the landscape and the life forms within it, and the human past, present, and future that make the preserve unique. Numerous original illustrations afford an immediate connection between the reader and the natural world just outside our door. The guidebook seeks to enhance understanding of that world and our role in preserving it for all time.

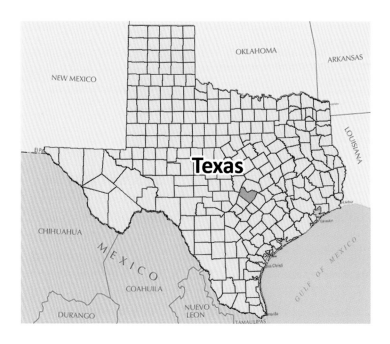

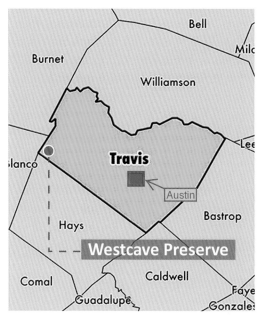

Westcave Preserve is located in westernmost Travis County, thirty miles west of downtown Austin. Maps by J. Robert Anderson and Zixu Qiao

INTRODUCTION

Westcave Preserve, the Crown Jewel of Central Texas

Westcave Preserve is located thirty miles west of downtown Austin among the rugged hills and deep valleys of the Texas Hill Country in central Texas. For forty years the preserve has inspired quiet reflection and enthusiasm from its visitors. Schoolchildren, families, casual hikers, and dedicated naturalists value and enjoy this idyllic refuge in far western Travis County and its award-winning, green-designed educational facility, the Warren Skaaren Environmental Learning Center.

The seventy-six-acre preserve is on two levels: a drier upland plateau (called the Uplands) typical of the Texas Hill Country, and a more moderate canyon of exceptional beauty with a clear, fast-flowing stream. The springwaters that sustain the stream cascade over a forty-foot-high waterfall into a deep emerald pool. Ornate deposits of travertine at the waterfall and along the canyon walls form columns and draperies that partly enclose a natural recess, creating the cave that gives the preserve its name.

Westcave Preserve's location—on the Central Flyway for bird migration and at the convergence of several plant communities in central Texas—contributes to its remarkable biodiversity. Through ongoing resource management, the land, water, and wide variety of plants and animals that take advantage of that biodiversity are well protected.

The visitor will find a system of nature trails through the Uplands property and a trail for guided hikes into the canyon. In addition, a solar observatory and other amazing exhibits built into the floor and walls of the Environmental Learning Center connect the visitor with the Sun, Earth's orbit, and the natural world outside. Westcave has won numerous international, national, and local awards for green building, resource protection, and excellence in environmental education. In addition, the preserve is a designated NASA environmental education facility and a component of the Balcones Canyonlands Preserve system of protected habitats for endangered species, as well as being the focus of various scientific research initiatives.

Established in 1976, Westcave Preserve is a privately maintained public-private partnership. The property is owned by the Lower Colorado River

Authority (LCRA), a public agency based in Austin that provides water and energy resource development and conservation. Westcave Preserve Corporation entered into two ninety-nine-year leases with the LCRA to manage the property and provide educational programming. Operations are governed by a board of directors supported by a professional staff and many dedicated volunteers, all working to implement the twin goals of natural area protection and lifetime environmental learning.

In 2013 Westcave Preserve Corporation announced a new name, Westcave Outdoor Discovery Center, to carry the message of conservation beyond the preserve's boundaries. Throughout this book, Westcave is used as a shorthand version of Westcave Outdoor Discovery Center, which encompasses all of the nonprofit's educational, conservation, and collaborative initiatives. Westcave Preserve, or the preserve, is used when referring to the nonprofit's land in western Travis County. Westcave is recognized nationally and internationally as both an ecological jewel and an innovator in promoting nature awareness and outdoor experience.

There is a lot to see and do at Westcave Preserve. Visitors of all ages are welcome. On weekdays the Uplands trails are open to the public for self-guided hiking, and school groups and other organizations use the preserve for tours and educational programs. On weekends, guided public tours of the canyon and grotto are available at specified times. Reservations are not accepted, but visitors should call ahead or consult the website to learn about special events and holiday and weather-related closings. There are picnic tables, restrooms, and drinking water on-site, but no food options. All amenities are available just a few miles away.

For more information about Westcave Outdoor Discovery Center, visit www.westcave.org. Telephone the preserve at (830) 825-3442 and the administrative offices at (512) 276-2257.

PART 1
Visitor's Guide

American Beautyberry (*Callicarpa americana*) with mature fruit. Illustration by Nancy McGowan

1 ❧ A WALK THROUGH THE PRESERVE

Out in the open on shelflike formations I found scattered specimens growing freely and, it seemed, miraculously out of a natural
pavement, surely an audacious invasion of enemy territory. Here,
blooming cheerily among the toughest and most presumptuous,
was the blue gilia, well named golden-eye, delicate and coquett-
ish. It does seem to be a miracle that from the bones of tiny organisms deposited millions of
years ago on the floor of an
ancient sea there should
now arise to greet the sun a
little flower marked by such
ingenious and beautiful
workmanship.

—Roy Bedichek, *Adventures
with a Texas Naturalist* (1947,
1975)

Splitleaf gilia
Giliastrum incisum
-NH-
2008

Splitleaf Gilia (*Giliastrum incisum*) graces the
Westcave landscape. Illustration by Nan Hampton

Deep in the heart of Texas
there is a place so unex-
pected, so inspiring,
that it steals your breath,
quickens your pulse, and
delights your senses. That
place is Westcave Preserve,
a seventy-six-acre nature
preserve and environmental
education facility in western Travis County. Lying
within the Hill Country,
the easternmost portion of
the Edwards Plateau, the

When walking through the preserve, leave only footprints, like everyone else.
Illustration by Rene Braud

preserve embraces the fauna and flora of five major ecological communities, resulting in extraordinary complexity. The preserve is at once a treasure trove of stunning beauty, biological wonders, and scientific fascination. Yet it is the amazing range of microenvironments—diversity in proximity—that makes the preserve unique:

- A level, stony upland, home to an oak–juniper–mixed grass savanna that is dry and seemingly austere but surprisingly rich and heterogeneous
- The steep, bedrock-walled valley of the Pedernales River, forming a nearly vertical arid land
- The slot canyon of Heinz Branch, which is moist, lush, and ten degrees cooler than its surroundings in summer
- Intermittent streams, carrying runoff and sediment, merging with spring flow to make lower Heinz Branch perennial
- A spectacular forty-foot waterfall cascading into the placid depths of a forty-foot-deep plunge pool

- A recessed cave that was the playground for the ancients and bygone generations of picnickers, swimmers, and campers
- Fern-covered travertine mounds and rock draperies, looming like medieval gargoyles from the canyon's cliffs or hanging like icicles beneath the waterfall, and
- A cave with rimstone dams and fossils on an ancient seabed and bristling with stalactites and stalagmites.

Begin your visit to the preserve's canyon by walking on flat upland terrain through a mosaic of wildflower meadows, luxuriant native grasslands, and old-growth woodlands of Ashe Juniper and Live Oak. Your plant list will include Black-foot Daisy and Huisache Daisy, Texas Grama and Sideoats Grama, Buckley's Yucca and Twisted-leaf Yucca, Lance-leaf Sumac and Aromatic Sumac—names that are the vernacular of botanists but for everyone else a kind of poetry. Many kinds of cactus—Lindheimer's Prickly Pear, Tasajillo, Claret Cup, and Lace Cactus—stand like coral patch reefs, each harboring communities of insects, reptiles, small mammals, and other plants.

A male Golden-cheeked Warbler (*Setophaga chrysoparia*) heralding spring. Photo © Michael A. Murphy

In springtime you may be treated to the polyphonous serenade of more than one hundred bird species led by the endangered Golden-cheeked Warbler. Watch your step: industrious Leafcutting Ants transport their booty across the path to enormous underground chambers where they grow fungus to feed their larvae.

The trail takes you to an overlook jutting above the precipitous valley wall of the Pedernales River. Treetops surround you at eye level. Across the valley, the landscape is stair-stepped, corresponding to differences in the types of bedrock at given elevations. Fractured limestone caps the valley walls and encompasses the sometimes peaceful, oft-times raging river, one of the last untamed waterways in Texas.

A little farther along the trail, you drop into a side canyon formed by Heinz Branch, a tributary of the Pedernales. As you climb sixty feet down a steep, 125-step stairway, part of which is carved into bedrock, you pass through layers of limestone 120 million years old. When these rocks were still soft sediment at the edge of a shallow sea, dinosaurs were alive and well, but whales, elephants, dogs, cats, chimpanzees, and humans had not yet evolved. Fractured and porous, the rock is clearly showing its age.

This limestone is known as the Cow Creek Formation, and it is an aquifer. Where aquifers lie deep underground, they are generally saturated with groundwater. Here, the upper part of this aquifer has been exposed by ero-

Texas Leafcutting Ant (*Atta texana*) carrying fruit of the American Beautyberry (*Callicarpa americana*). Photo © Michael A. Murphy

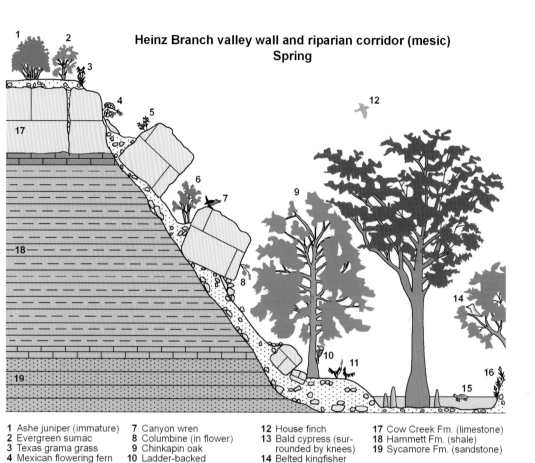

Heinz Branch valley wall and riparian corridor (mesic)
Spring

1 Ashe juniper (immature)	**7** Canyon wren	**12** House finch	**17** Cow Creek Fm. (limestone)
2 Evergreen sumac	**8** Columbine (in flower)	**13** Bald cypress (surrounded by knees)	**18** Hammett Fm. (shale)
3 Texas grama grass	**9** Chinkapin oak		**19** Sycamore Fm. (sandstone)
4 Mexican flowering fern	**10** Ladder-backed woodpecker	**14** Belted kingfisher	
5 Alabama lipfern	**11** Green dragon (in flower)	**15** Red-eared slider	
6 Mexican buckeye		**16** Horsetail	

Heinz Branch wall and its moister riverbank habitats, with typical fauna and flora (in spring). Illustration by S. Christopher Caran and Joel Lardon

sion, allowing much of the water to drain away. The rock remains porous, however, and at least six species of fern grow along the stairway, sustained by rainwater seeping through the cracks and cavities in the rock. The trail affords a remarkable perspective: you see the aquifer from the inside. You are looking at the subterranean pathways that allow the aquifer to transmit groundwater.

Continuing your descent, you approach Heinz Branch, the perennial stream that has for thousands of years carved this canyon ever deeper, ever longer. Massive Bald Cypress trees line the banks, their roots buried in the wet soil they require. Curious projections known as knees grow upward from the roots, rising above ground and thus facilitating gas exchange needed for photosynthesis. The trees are huge, their branches spanning the canyon, their leaf canopy and the sheltering cliffs enveloping you in a natural terrarium. Unlike other conifers such as pine and spruce, cypress trees lose their needlelike leaves in autumn, allowing sunlight to reach the canyon floor throughout the winter months.

In spring, new leaves emerge, signaling a return to the seasons of plenty. By summer the canyon's leaf cover provides shade. Evaporative cooling

Maidenhair Fern (*Adiantum capillus-veneris*). Photo by Ron Sprouse

A Note about Butterflies of Westcave Preserve

Approximately sixty species of butterflies are seen regularly in the preserve, and more than thirty additional species have been observed in the general area. Some, like the Spicebush Swallowtail (*Papilio troilus*), are at the western limit of their range. There is a group of spring butterflies that fly in that season and no other. Among these are the delicate Falcate Orangetip (*Anthocharis midea*), which is often seen nectaring on Bluebonnets. During the fall, unusual vagrant species wander north from the Rio Grande Valley and Mexico, adding to the diversity of species in the preserve. May and October are the peak months for sighting butterflies.

Many of the preserve's plants serve as food for adult butterflies or their caterpillars. The preserve has two principal habitats: the Uplands with Live Oak–Ashe Juniper savannas, and the canyon with its deep shade and perennial stream. Plants in the Uplands are dependent on adequate rain, whereas the protected canyon enjoys a constant water supply that maintains a number of plants in most seasons.

Adult butterflies are often seen nectaring on flowers, but most of their time is spent locating mates, courting, and looking for plants on which to lay eggs. Adults feed on many sorts of flowers, but the caterpillars are typically specialists dining on one or a small group of plants called the host plants (see butterfly list in Appendix E).

The relationship between plant and insect is crucial to understanding butterfly ecology. After several weeks of feeding, the caterpillar changes into an immobile resting state, called the chrysalis. With several more weeks of internal reorganization, the metamorphosis is complete, and the adult butterfly emerges. This life cycle can occur in as little as four to six weeks. Most species can complete two or three life cycles between spring and fall, but a few species have a single brood per year, usually in spring.

The preserve's signature butterfly is the Spicebush Swallowtail, which is here because the moist soil near the creek in the canyon supports a dense colony of Spicebush plants (*Lindera benzoin*), the host plant for this butterfly. The leaves produce chemicals that give off a fragrant smell but are toxic to most herbivores. The Spicebush Swallowtail caterpillar can eat the leaves because it has evolved the ability to tolerate or detoxify the chemical repellent.

The Spicebush plant's stronghold is in east Texas, but there are a few canyons in the Texas Hill Country that have conditions favorable to its growth. The large swallowtail floats slowly through the canyon shadows, males looking for females and females looking for plants for their eggs. The adult male is dark black with a greenish blue sheen on its hindwing. The female's colors are more muted. After hatching, the young Spicebush caterpillar constructs a shelter at the end of a Spicebush leaf folded lengthwise. The caterpillar occupies this shelter as it matures. With its leaf green color and two eyelike spots, the caterpillar may resemble a green snake as it pokes its head out of the shelter to startle would-be predators.

Another special tree in the canyon is the Redbay, a species commonly found 150 miles away in eastern and coastal Texas. Caterpillars of Henry's Elfin (*Callophrys henrici*), a spring butterfly, are often found in Redbays. Another butterfly, the Palamedes Swallowtail (*Papilio palamedes*), uses the Redbay as its host plant. This beautiful swallowtail has not been reported at the preserve yet, but it may be present at least occasionally, since the butterfly has been found at nearby Hamilton Pool Preserve.

The Spicebush and Redbay plants are only two examples of relict plant populations that survive from an earlier climate regime when these plants were more widespread. The Hill Country canyons offer many examples of plants now separated from their primary home ranges by hundreds of miles. As you walk through Westcave Preserve, think about the ecological link between these unique plants and the unique butterflies that depend on them.

reduces the air temperature perceptibly, whereas in winter the microclimate is stabilized by protection from the wind and by the humidity and constant temperature of emerging springwaters. The wetter environment of the canyon differs markedly from the drier Uplands just a short distance above. This range of variation makes Westcave Preserve a botanical paradise supporting more than four hundred plant species. Within the canyon—and only within the canyon—are Chatterbox Orchid, Spicebush, Green Dragon, Chinkapin Oak, Horsetail, and Redbay. Butterflies also abound. Some form intimate partnerships with the plants, either as unique pollinators or as the adult phases of caterpillars that feed on the leaves of only one species.

Near the canyon floor the trail turns upstream beneath a bower of vines. Some have names that are picturesque and even amusing: Mustang Grape, Pearl Milkweed Vine, Bracted Passionflower, Bearded Swallow-wort, and Cow-itch Vine. Other names provide lessons in geography and history: Alabama Supplejack, Carolina Snailseed, Virginia Creeper, Texas Bindweed, and Alamo Vine. As you walk on, stepping across rivulets of springwater and squeezing past enormous blocks of limestone fallen from the canyon rim, Columbine, Roemer's Sage, and Maidenhair Fern grow from tiny depressions on the surfaces of these boulders amid mosses, lichens, and liverworts.

Look about you. There is verdure in every shade and every direction. Take time to explore. Let the falling notes of the Canyon Wren, White-eyed Vireo, Eastern Phoebe, and Yellow-billed Cuckoo set your pace. The canyon narrows just ahead, forming a natural amphitheater or grotto. You are surrounded by green, as if the walls were cut jade. Then you see the waterfall. Its beauty is astonishing, yet engaging and personal. Perhaps you heard the falls before they came into view. After a rainstorm, billowing sheets of water plummet from the falls with a deafening roar. The plunging water gouges and abrades the stream bed, producing a deep, clear pool. Floods caused by especially heavy rains sometimes refill the pool with sediment, only to scour it clean some other day.

From time to time floods have stripped much of the vegetation from the stream channel and canyon floor. The salutary environmental conditions and natural resilience of this diverse yet closely integrated biotic community soon restore the flora to its former glory. The canyon is insulated from extreme winter temperatures, but when plants are affected, this damage, too, is temporary. Rarely, an ironbound cold night produces a truly ethereal spectacle: falling water transformed to ice. See it in the first rays of dawn, for this crystalline display is as fleeting as a dream.

The waterfall flows year-round. Yet long after a rain you may notice that water is not coming from the normally dry stream channel above the falls, but from springs at the waterfall's brink. Springwaters emerge from beds of hard limestone at the base of the Cow Creek aquifer. These beds are so hard that they form the roof of a deeply recessed rock shelter below and behind the falls. There is a distinct contrast between the erosion-resistant Cow Creek Formation and the underlying Hammett Shale, which is soft and unstable when exposed. Rapid weathering of the Hammett Shale has undercut the Cow Creek limestone, producing both the rock shelter and the waterfall.

Eventually, undercutting will advance too far and the overhanging limestone bed will collapse. Huge, angular boulders can be seen at the falls and at points downstream that were the locations of waterfalls in earlier times. As each waterfall collapsed, stream flow, selective erosion, and spring discharge combined to create a new falls just upstream. This process has been ongoing for millennia and is the primary mechanism by which Heinz Branch has incised and lengthened its canyon.

A footbridge conveys the hiking trail across the stream. Near the waterfall, the trail forks. To the left is a short, steep segment extending behind the falls. Long before there was a preserve, this part of the trail was cut into the rock by hand. At the end of the trail your view is immediately drawn to the water pouring from the heart of the aquifer. Here, groundwater becomes surface water in a rushing tumble of liquid diamonds.

Because water is magical, there is another transformation in store: nature performs a sublime alchemy, turning water into stone. Within the aquifer, minerals dissolved from the surrounding limestone enrich the water. A chemist would call this water supersaturated. As the springwater emerges from its underground confines, the surrounding pressure and temperature change abruptly. This effect is further enhanced by turbulence as the water tumbles over the falls and down the sloping rocks below.

Under these new conditions, the dissolved minerals can no longer remain in solution. What the water takes from the limestone it must give back in kind. Limestone is primarily composed of the mineral calcite, and each gallon of springwater deposits a microscopic film of calcite crystals on everything it touches. Gradually, with the passage of millions of gallons, the crystal film becomes either a thick layer or an enormous column of rock. This special rock, called travertine, is moderately hard yet porous and layered. In the dim light behind the falls, mosses grow on the still-wet travertine, forming small hummocks called tuft mounds. The surface of these mounds is soft, but just below we find that the moss filaments have turned to stone, literally petrified in place as the travertine hardens.

Leaves falling from trees above the falls often come to rest on the travertine mound. The just-fallen leaves are still flexible, but within days they become rigid and firmly attached to the underlying mound. This is fossilization, but at an accelerated pace, occurring right before your eyes. The leaves, mosses, dead insects, microscopic organisms—even occasional feathers—are perfectly preserved. An ancient travertine deposit is like a crystal ball: by peering into it, we can see into the distant past to learn what organisms lived here.

The right-hand fork of the trail leads to a short flight of stairs and a cave. As you climb, look above and around you. A curtain of travertine deposited by other springs along the grotto's rim has enclosed part of the overhang, forming a cave. It is surprisingly dark, but as your eyes become accustomed you see stalactites, stalagmites, columns, and tiny, stair-stepped pools. All are fresh with newly accreted calcite from water dripping through the ceiling.

The entire ceiling is a single bed of limestone, cantilevered and self-supporting despite a network of fine cracks. Look up and you will see the shells of fossil oysters, calling cards from the time when this part of central Texas was an ocean. Archeological remains—stone artifacts used as tools, weapons, and domestic goods—have been found in the cave, recording the presence of Native Americans. There are other reminders of a more recent past: an inscription near the cave entrance identifies a sightseer who came here in the late 1800s.

Clearly, Westcave Preserve has long attracted admirers. In a way, each visitor leaves a mark. Graffiti is no longer permitted, nor is the disposal of modern artifacts. Footprints fade away, as do the echoes of laughter, curious inquiries, and expressions of awe. What remains is an invisible armor, fashioned from a common resolve that the preserve must forever be what it is today: a constant place of exquisite perfection, but always displaying something new. Your memories ensure your commitment to this principle, and Westcave Preserve will always welcome you.

2 ❧ VISITOR CENTER AND INDOOR EXHIBITS

[We choose] to build only structures which are undeniably essential, and to know that [the architect] is not equipped to embellish, but only to mar, Nature's better canvases. Now and forever, the degree of his success within such areas will be measurable by the yardstick of his self-restraint.

—*Albert H. Good, Park and Recreation Structures (1938)*

The Warren Skaaren Environmental Learning Center (ELC) is a place for gathering, collaborating, learning, discovery, and investigation. It is named for screenwriter Warren Skaaren (*Top Gun, Beverly Hills Cop II, Beetlejuice,* and *Batman*), whose charitable trust made the first large donation to the ELC building fund. Its ingenious design presents learning opportunities, helping visitors understand the natural forces of water, sky, and land around them.

Designed by Robert Jackson, FAIA, of Jackson & McElhaney Architects, Austin, Texas, the ELC has won seven major design awards, most notably the 2005 Award of Excellence from the American Institute of Architects Committee on Architecture for Education (AIA/CAE). In 2006 the AIA named the ELC one of the top ten "green" buildings in the United States.

The site was selected by John Ahrns (resident manager) and the board to have a minimal impact on the ecology of the preserve. Throughout construction, project partners upheld high standards of care for the land. The design process lasted nearly five years—much longer than normal—while the project was funded, giving "time to refine the ideas," said Jackson: "The design was truly a collaboration among us and John Ahrns, the Board (99 percent was E. Lee Walker, chairman/inspirer), the Lower Colorado River Authority and the site."

The Warren Skaaren Environmental Learning Center (ELC) seen from the south patio. Photo by Greg Hursley

The ELC was dedicated on March 21, 2003, the spring (vernal) equinox. During the dedication ceremony a male Golden-cheeked Warbler chose that moment to linger on a perch above the main speaker and deliver his own buzzy message. Another buzz arose—this one from the audience—as they noticed the outspoken presence of the endangered bird that nests at the preserve in the spring.

More than one hundred thousand students and visitors have taken part in Westcave's environmental education tours and programs since 1976. The ELC is now the gathering place for most of these activities and also offers space for community meetings, including the Westcave Roundtable, a group of more than one hundred neighbors representing approximately twenty thousand acres of land who are interested in the conservation of the lower Pedernales River and surrounding area.

Architect Jackson started from the premise that "it's impossible to

Connecting kids with nature comes to life with the visit of a Common Gray Fox (*Urocyon cinereoargenteus*)just outside the ELC. Photo by Erich Rose

improve on nature." He said it was "worrying to build in a preserve" and looked for inspiration to the structures built by the Civilian Conservation Corps in parks around the country during the Great Depression of the 1930s and to the stories of how architecture connects us to the natural world. Jackson concluded that he needed to create an object of beauty, yet make it as much an actual part of the natural world as possible. He created a 3,000-square-foot building with another 4,000 square feet of outdoor classroom under roofs or trellises, including a 1,750-square-foot terrace overlooking the Pedernales River canyon. "It's a gateway, a landing site for this spectacular place," said Jackson.

ELC Exhibits

In addition to being a showcase for green building design principles, within and around the ELC are a series of educational exhibits intended to engage and inform visitors of all ages and connect them with the outside world they have come to see. Each exhibit illustrates a separate facet of the natural world and its intimate effects on all of us.

Solar Observatory

The ELC houses a remarkable solar observatory so awe-inspiring that architect Jackson has been called on to create others in schools and private homes. Jackson found inspiration for this simple yet striking feature during a visit to the Basilica of Saint Mary of the Angels and the Martyrs in Rome. That solar observatory, in which is laid out a meridian line, was designed by Francesco Bianchini for Pope Clement XI in the early 1700s, in part to accurately predict the date for Easter.

Students investigate the Solar Observatory in the ELC. Photo by Ron Sprouse

Look up from inside the ELC and think of the broad arc of the roof as the dome of the sky. Notice the words "Sol Omnibus Lucet" (the Sun shines on everything) inscribed around the solar window, a small hole in the roof. The sunlight admitted through this opening appears as a spot of light that, as the Earth turns, unfailingly moves down the west wall and across the floor each day when the sky is clear. This sun spot advances toward a meridian line in the floor—a twenty-eight-foot-long narrow plate with tick marks for each day of the year. The calendar is precisely aligned with the north-south orientation of the building. Designed in collaboration with Dan Lester of the University of Texas Department of Astronomy, Westcave's Solar Observatory is accurate within one second, confirmed by an atomic clock.

The relationship between the Earth and the Sun is one of the most important cycles of nature. To watch the spot of sunlight move is to watch the Earth spin and move around the Sun, or, put another way, to experience the apparent motion of the Sun across the sky. Throughout history, many

Sol omnibus lucet: The Sun shines on everything. The solar window in the roof and ceiling of the ELC allows entry of a spot of sunlight that crosses the solar observatory each day, weather permitting. Photo by Addie Louise Broussard

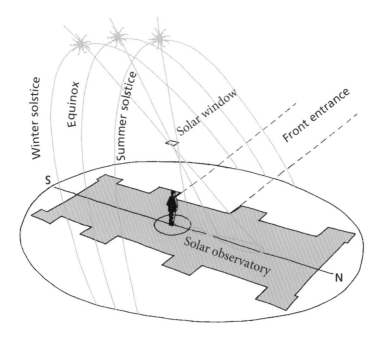

Orientation of the solar window and solar observatory, illustrating the daily arc of the sun across the sky at different seasons. Illustration by Drew Patterson and Linda Wofford

different cultures have used the Sun's motion to keep track of the date and time and to maintain a calendar so they would know when to plant crops and celebrate holidays.

Every day the shaft of sunlight crosses the calendar at that date's mark. During the year, the sun spot will cross the northernmost end of the calendar on the day of December's winter solstice, corresponding to the Sun's most southerly arc across the sky. The spot crosses the southernmost end of the calendar on June's summer solstice, related to the sun's most northerly arc. There also are tick marks on the calendar for the equinoxes in March and September. As you look at the calendar plate, note the tip of the hat to the preserve's late resident manager, John Ahrns, whose birthday is celebrated with his name next to the tick mark for February 24.

Just for fun, the spot of sunlight crossing the meridian line has been rigged to power a photovoltaic strip, causing the first few bars of the Beatles' "Here Comes the Sun" to play. This feature delights visitors so much that docents and staff usually seize the moment to offer a more precise explanation of the solar observatory, which involves a description of the analemma, a figure eight that entwines the calendar plate. The analemma's shape projects a graph of the Earth's elliptic orbit, illustrating the changing relative speed of the Earth in its trip around the Sun. While the solar calendar can be used to determine the date, the analemma can be used to show the time of day precisely. Every day of the year, the spot of sunlight will cross the analemma at "mean local noon" (the moment when the Sun is halfway between rising and setting). The actual time of mean local noon depends on where you are on the Earth and occurs at 12:32:34 Central Standard Time at the preserve.

Horizons Sky Map

A large circle scribed into the floor at the south end of the Solar Observatory is a map illustrating the apparent motion of the Sun during the year. Visitors can use the sky map to situate themselves on this particular piece of land and relate its place under the changing sky. By standing in the middle of the large circle facing north (look for "YOU ARE HERE" at your feet), the visitor will see where the Sun rises (in the east, on your right) and sets (in the west, on your left) during the various months, which are written at the edge of the circle. Visitors also may calculate the angle of the Sun at any time of day, using a cursor with nine evenly spaced marks of 10 degrees.

The sun spot crosses a line called the analemma each day at Westcave Preserve's mean local noon: 12:32:34 pm Central Standard Time. Photo by Elaine Davenport

Nature's Numbers

Embedded in the floor at the south end of the ELC is a spiral inspired by the work of Fibonacci, a thirteenth-century mathematician. Through the spiral, even those visitors who profess to hate math, especially geometry, can see the beauty of numbers and how they help us understand the natural

Sky map at the southern end of the solar observatory. Photo by Greg Hursley

world. Lee Walker, Westcave board chair from 1980 to 2008 and a professed "math geek," has stated that the ELC is "perhaps the most intelligent building I've ever been in or heard of."

To illustrate Fibonacci's number sequence, the spiral on the floor is drawn by using squares as building blocks. The dimensions of the squares

Students learn about nature's numbers by aligning along the Fibonacci spiral in the floor of the ELC. Photo by Ron Sprouse

are in the proportions of successive Fibonacci numbers—a sequence, beginning with one, in which each number in succession is equal to the sum of the two previous numbers (1+0=1, 1+1=2, 2+1=3, 3+2=5, 5+3=8, 8+5=13, 13+8=21, etc.). The resulting spiral that encloses the squares is nearly identical to the spirals that occur in plants and animals, such as the curving horns of bighorn sheep, the ninety-million-year-old ammonite embedded in the ELC floor, ocean waves, and our spiral galaxy. Note also that many plants and animals (pinecones and starfish, for example) have 3 or 5 or 8 or 21 parts—all Fibonacci numbers.

The Fibonacci sequence also is related to the common and visually pleasing Golden Rectangle. The ratio of the lengths of the long and short sides of the rectangle is in approximately the same proportion as any two consecutive Fibonacci numbers. For example, the ratio of the successive Fibonacci numbers 5 and 3 (5 divided by 3 = 1.667) is similar to the rectangle's proportions, 1.618. The Golden Rectangle can be used to describe the dimensions of many birds' eggs, the delicate symmetry of butterfly wings, and the shape of salt crystals and is widely used in art, architecture, and many common objects such as the rectangle of a credit card.

Look around you and note that the geometry of the Golden Rectangle is used to shape spaces within the Environmental Learning Center. The Fibonacci sequence and the Golden Rectangle describe beautiful shapes that recur in nature, showing how extraordinarily beautiful math can be.

North Star and Latitude

At the far north end of the ELC, another floor exhibit illustrates that in the Northern Hemisphere the latitude of a location on the Earth's surface is approximately equal to the altitude of Polaris, the North Star, above the horizon. Polaris is the axis spot in the sky about which the stars appear to revolve. At night, if you stand at this exhibit, the North Star is visible just below the curve of the arching roof. Of course, the North Star is there during the day, too, but cannot be seen.

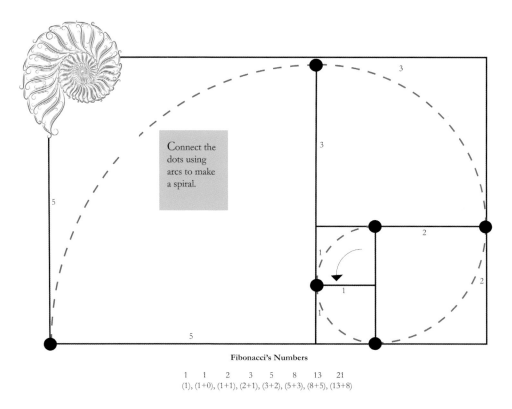

Connect the dots using arcs to make a spiral.

Fibonacci's Numbers

1   1   2   3   5   8   13   21
(1), (1+0), (1+1), (2+1), (3+2), (5+3), (8+5), (13+8)

Nature's numbers and the Fibonacci spiral. Illustration by Linda Wofford based on an image by Drew Patterson. Nautilus from iStock.com/Lonely

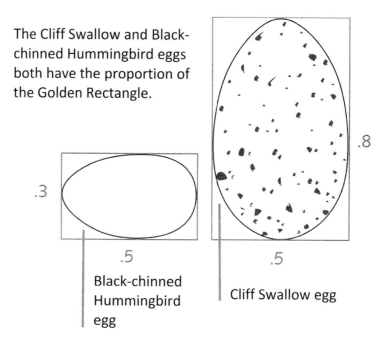

The Cliff Swallow and Black-chinned Hummingbird eggs both have the proportion of the Golden Rectangle.

.8

.3

.5

Black-chinned Hummingbird egg

.5

Cliff Swallow egg

The mathematical proportion of the Golden Rectangle can be applied to bird eggs. Illustration by Drew Patterson

Evolution of Westcave Preserve (Geology Panels)

Four graphic panels mounted on the exterior east wall of the ELC have been a permanent feature of the building since the beginning. The panels include illustrations and text describing changes in the landscape, starting 250,000 years ago, then 100,000 and 50,000 years ago, and at the present. (See chapter 8, "Evolution of Westcave Preserve.") The illustrations show the Pedernales River and the formation of the grotto in the Heinz Branch box canyon. These panels are the first stop on each guided canyon tour for school groups and weekend visitors.

Fossils of Texas

The ELC's visual delights include more than eighty fossils built into both the inside and outside walls. A number of the fossils are loose specimens that were pressed into the mortar joints, and others are actually in the quarried stone. Some of those specimens are unusual and even rare. They include several fish with obvious scales, jawbones, and teeth.

The rocks that make up the landscape of the Hill Country were laid down as sediment in a shallow sea about 110 million to 120 million years ago.

Those rocks are well known to paleontologists for the rich record of ancient life to be found in them in the form of fossils. Shells, casts, teeth, bones, and even the footprints of dinosaurs can be found throughout central Texas. The stone and associated fossils of the ELC were all quarried from layers of the Glen Rose Formation near Sisterdale in Kendall County, Texas. The quarry was owned by Ray Smith, who for many years had set aside prime specimens, not finding a use for them until Westcave Preserve wanted limestone for its new building, at which time Smith realized he had found the perfect home for the fossils he had kept aside.

Representative specimens of fossils that can be collected in central Texas are in a display case inside the ELC donated in 1996 by the Central Texas Paleontological Society. The fossils range in age from the Eocene Epoch (56 to 34 million years ago) to the Pennsylvanian Period (323 to 300 million years ago), although the majority are from the Cretaceous Period (145 to 66 million years ago).

Ammonite fossil from the Cretaceous Period embedded in the exterior wall on the southeastern side of the ELC. Photo by Elaine Davenport

In 2006 the Central Texas Paleontological Society merged with the Austin Paleontological Society to form the Paleontological Society of Austin. The fossil collection at Westcave Preserve is of such merit that the society holds its annual picnic and auction at the ELC and continues to maintain and upgrade the display.

Artifact Display Case

Another small display case in the ELC is filled with a variety of objects that were collected from the preserve or nearby by the late John Ahrns, the preserve's first and longtime resident manager, and his son, Jeff Ahrns. The objects range from ancient stone tools and shards to coins and a rusty old spur. Above the case, and associated with it, can be found reproduction bows, arrows in a quiver, throwing darts (short spearlike objects), and an atlatl used to throw them, made and donated by Frank Harrison, an Ahrns family friend.

The Library

A small collection of books, some donated by the Tapestry Foundation of Austin, is available to visitors for reading or reference. Books and pamphlets on a variety of subjects, mostly nature and Texas history, are located on bookshelves designed and built by University of Texas architecture students. The field guides are often used by staff, volunteers, or visitors to identify something observed at the preserve. Books on history and local culture as well as a large variety of children's books can be read while awaiting the next scheduled tour.

Discovery Trunks

Several rolling wooden trunks display specimens and objects pertaining to a number of subjects. A geology-themed trunk includes specimens of the various types of rocks found at the preserve, including a sectioned stalagmite from the cave. Pull-out display drawers show typical fossils of the region.

Another trunk features mounted skulls of typical Hill Country mammals. Display drawers feature scat, tracks, and the bones of some smaller vertebrates, including snakes. At the bottom of the trunk, six concealed objects invite visitors to reach in, touch, and guess what is inside. Another trunk is all about the preserve's smaller inhabitants, including plants, insects, and birds. Graphics on each trunk put the objects and specimens into context.

Photos and Drawings

A display of framed photographs covers the east wall in the south classroom. Taken by local photographers, including Ronald Sprouse and Michael A. Murphy, the images include flora and fauna of the preserve. The display includes several photos of the preserve before and after floods as well as enlarged images of male and female endangered Golden-cheeked Warblers. These photos give visitors an idea of what to expect when exploring the preserve. In the north classroom a number of black-and-white historical photos can be found as well as drawings by artist Nancy McGowan depicting several of the preserve's flora and fauna.

Media Station

A large monitor provides a set of looping video clips on the preserve and its ongoing research projects. Clips from various news stations and self-produced promotions are featured. During once-a-month astronomy events, the display is connected to ViewSpace/SkyWatch and receives a direct feed from the Space Telescope Science Institute, which provided the display and associated hardware and software in 2006. Westcave Preserve is one of the select video feed stations for educational programming related to astronomy and space exploration for the National Aeronautics and Space Administration (NASA).

The Building

The stone used in the walls of the building is Glen Rose limestone, from a quarry near Sisterdale, Texas. Because it contains a small quantity of iron, the stone has an attractive rosy glow. This is the stone in which tracks of Texas dinosaurs have been found in many locations and is a favorite of kids. Note that the size of the stone used in the walls diminishes towards the ceiling, representing the breaking of rock layers by plants and weathering over time—the top thin and layered, the middle beginning to break up, and the base consisting of large chunks. The stone was chosen because the stair-stepped hills around the preserve are of the Glen Rose Formation, thus blending the building with the natural world just outside.

Green Building Design

In 2006, the American Institute of Architects selected the ELC as one of the top ten "green" buildings in the United States. Green buildings utilize water and energy efficiently and generally provide spaces for living and work that require minimal maintenance. To control the effects of direct solar exposure, green buildings usually feature the longer perimeter walls along the north and south sides. Because the site of the ELC imposed limitations, the long walls are on the east and west. However, other aspects of green design were maximized:

- By opening windows at ground level and in the cupola above, the ELC can benefit from the chimney effect and realize a ten-degree temperature differential as air is drawn through and upward.
- The Sun's path and position were assessed to produce the correct width of roof overhangs (eight feet on both the east and west sides) to prevent the Sun from directly shining on windows during the summer but to allow sunlight to penetrate during the winter.
- Clerestory windows all around the building maximize natural light and reduce electrical use.
- Insulation is R-30 recycled cardboard.
- A metal, two-inch standing seam roof is shaped to maximize rainwater collection.
- The building frame is recycled steel.
- The foundation is concrete containing approximately 25 percent fly ash content instead of the usual 20 percent, thus increasing the use of recycled materials. Fly ash is ash and soot that accumulates inside the stacks of coal-burning power plants.
- The ceiling is untreated loblolly pine from East Texas installed in a tongue-and-groove fashion. This design is typical of historic structures in the region. As the building heats and cools, the wood undergoes slight changes in shape, making itself known with popping sounds, surprising and even delighting visitors.
- The roof, gutters, scuppers, and rainwater tanks mimic the natural watershed. The roof is comparable to the surface watershed and the gutters to creeks, and the scuppers shoot water to the rainwater tanks just as water in nature is funneled underground to the aquifer (water table). Note the hammered copper scuppers—works of art in themselves.

Other Features

"Are those gun ports in the wall?" is a common question from visitors. The narrow, recessed sun slots through the west wall and about forty inches off the ground are a reminder of the land's position on the planet and the changing seasons. The slots and building are astronomically aligned so that light is channeled into the building near sunset on the summer and winter solstices and the spring and fall equinoxes. Jackson's inspiration came from the sunlight slots at Hovenweep Castle, a building of an ancient Puebloan civilization in southeast Utah.

The south end of the ELC doubles as an indoor classroom that can be partitioned with glass doors to create two acoustically separate spaces. There also are two covered outdoor classrooms, one on the south and one on the north side of the building.

Terrazzo is a major component of the floor. It is lighter colored to the east of the meridian line (ante meridiem, AM) where the Sun rises, and darker colored on the west side of the meridian line (post meridiem, PM) where the Sun sets. Another part of the interior flooring is Oklahoma Sugarloaf sandstone, used in a flagstone pattern. Under the building, sealed pipes carry water at a temperature of 68°F, pumped from five three-hundred-foot-deep wells. The water circulation provides cooling in the summer and heating in the winter.

Outside the south end of the building are solar panels that can send up to two thousand watts of energy into the power grid.

For its sanitary services, the preserve uses two Clivus Multrum composting toilets, which use neither water nor chemicals. They rely on the ability of bacteria and atmospheric oxygen to decompose the solid waste. The self-sanitized waste can then be used as compost for plants. Septic fields and a reconstructed wetland, where native aquatic plants and bacteria act to clean the water, handle the other waste water from sinks at the restrooms and ELC and from the kitchen and bathrooms of the residence.

Rainwater collected from the ELC roof is stored in limestone-clad holding tanks at the north and south ends of the building and is used to fill the south pond and irrigate the xeriscaped native plantings. Famed horticulturist Jill Nokes designed the landscaping. The pond contains native aquatic plants, fish, and insects and is a favorite of birds.

3 ❧ TRAILS AND OUTDOOR FEATURES

Most of Westcave Preserve consists of vegetated natural space, and to allow access to those areas, two trail systems have been developed. The Canyon Trail, which has been open since the preserve was created and is now named for John Covert Watson, begins at the Environmental Learning Center (ELC) and descends into the Heinz Branch canyon. The trail is dedicated to Watson, who had the foresight to first buy what would become Westcave Preserve in 1974 and then initiate the establishment of the nonprofit Westcave Preserve Corporation in 1976.

The Uplands trail system also begins at the ELC but stays on the higher Live Oak–Ashe Juniper savanna. Although only guided tours are allowed on the Canyon Trail, the Uplands trails are open to self-guided exploration, but to protect the environment, some restrictions apply.

Westcave grotto. Photo © Michael A. Murphy/TxDOT

John Covert Watson Canyon Trail

The Canyon Trail tour begins on the rim of the canyon in a semiarid plateau typical of the Texas Hill Country. A short walk through the oak-juniper plateau landscape provides an introduction to that habitat and an overview of the Pedernales River valley. The trail then descends 125 steep steps through a limestone crevice into the sheltered canyon of Heinz Branch. The trail continues alongside a flowing stream with lush plant life and ends at the head of the canyon, where a forty-foot waterfall replenishes an emerald pool. Decorating the grotto area is travertine, a mineral substance much like stalactites and stalagmites. The travertine has formed columns and draperies that partly enclose a natural recess, creating the cave that gives Westcave Preserve its name.

Guided tours are offered on weekends at 10 a.m., noon, 2 p.m., and 4 p.m. Bad weather or special events may alter the schedule, so check beforehand at www.westcave.org. There is a fee for the one-mile roundtrip walk,

The Ahrns Bench was dedicated in 2010 to recognize the many contributions of John Ahrns, "The Rock of Westcave", on his retirement as resident manager (1974 to 2010). Photo by Blaine T. Williams

Another inscription on the Ahrns Bench is by John Muir, acclaimed naturalist and writer. Photo by Blaine T. Williams

which starts at the Environmental Learning Center and lasts about ninety minutes.

To honor John Ahrns, the preserve's first and longtime resident manager, a bench was dedicated in 2010, the year Ahrns retired, at a rest stop on the plateau just before the main trail drops into the canyon. The three huge pieces of Glen Rose limestone, one placed as a bench and two upright, came from the same quarry in Sisterdale, Texas, that provided stone for the Environmental Learning Center. The bench features an inscription, a quotation from naturalist John Muir: "In every walk with nature one receives far more than he seeks." At the dedication ceremony, Ahrns, who was legendary for his entertaining and informative tours, was toasted by Westcave Executive Director Molly Stevens: "To John, for all of us who received so much more from a walk with you than we ever imagined possible."

The Uplands Trail System

Across from the ELC entrance is a wheelchair- and stroller-friendly raised boardwalk that goes by a Chimney Swift Tower and leads to the Uplands. The Uplands comprise forty-five acres of property purchased in 2008 to expand the preserve's mission of conservation, education, and stewardship. Conservation efforts on the Uplands, upstream from the waterfall and grotto, are essential to the health and function of the entire preserve. The area protects the water quality and provides a natural buffer against development and noise for the canyon below. In addition, the Uplands are an important natural resource in their own right, preserving oak-juniper woodlands, grasslands, and small segments of the Heinz Branch channel and watershed as well as historic structures.

The hard work of volunteers has been especially important to establishing and enhancing this piece of the preserve. Led by Land Manager Amber Ahrns Gosselin, a team was formed to learn about the land and develop a plan for its use. Volunteer scientists and naturalists came together in order to gain a holistic understanding of the acreage before visitor access was planned. Expert volunteers conducted so-called BioBlitzes to survey all plants and wildlife, plus the land's geologic, hydrologic, and archeological features. Input also came from focus groups and land management experts. The land use plan calls for more projects and improvements that will connect the visiting public with nature while minimizing adverse impacts to native flora and fauna.

The Uplands trail system was opened in March 2014 and is available

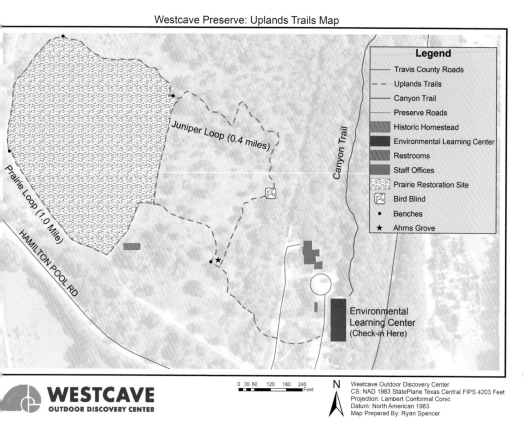

Map of the Uplands trails at Westcave Preserve. Map by Ryan Spencer

to the public for self-guided hiking during the week as well as weekends. Again, special circumstances may alter the usual schedule, so check beforehand at www.westcave.org. Systems are in place to monitor the impact of visitors so that changes can be made if necessary to maintain a balance between protection and visitor access.

Chimney Swift Tower

Along the path that leads to the Uplands, visit the fifteen-foot-tall Chimney Swift Tower, vital to the nesting and survival of Chimney Swifts (*Chaetura pelagica*).* If you hear a whooshing sound, a swift may be coming or going from the tower. Or you may hear a gentle chippering as they socialize with one another in the roost during nest building and at night. Interpretive panels are located on the tower.

Take this path to the Uplands, passing by the Chimney Swift Tower. Photo by Elaine Davenport

Ahrns Grove

At the end of the path leading to the Uplands trails is the Ahrns Grove, dedicated to the Ahrns family. The grove features native trees that were purchased with donations to Westcave in their honor when John Ahrns retired as resident manager in 2010. John and Brenda Ahrns lived at Westcave Preserve from 1974 to 2010, and their children, Jeff and Amber, lived on-site until their graduation from high school. More trees were planted in 2014 in memory of Ahrns, who died that year. Among the trees are an Eve's Necklace, a lesser known tree and one of Ahrns's favorites (as he said, "because it is obscure"); a Mexican Plum, which Ahrns liked because it smelled like a tortilla; and a Texas Redbud, the flowers of which Ahrns would use in the early spring as a topping on ice cream. A Monarch butterfly way station is also part of the Ahrns grove.

At Ahrns Grove is an interpretive display that serves as a jumping off point for the Uplands. It provides a map and information on wildlife. The trails wind through a Live Oak–Ashe Juniper savanna that provides essential habitat to a variety of wildlife. Choose either the 0.4-mile Juniper Loop, which is more shaded, or the 1-mile Prairie Loop, which is more open.

Scrub Live Oaks (*Quercus fusiformis*) and prairie grasses form the Uplands savanna habitat. Spring adds Bluebonnets (*Lupinus texensis*). Photo by Traci Ibarra

Bird Blinds

There are two bird blinds on the Uplands, each with a water feature, a bird guide, and a visitor log. Both afford excellent opportunities to observe and learn about the preserve's wide variety of birds. These blinds were made possible by the generous contributions of two neighborhood families—the Murphy family and Patti and David Boyd.

Historic Homestead

Just off the trail is the Historic Homestead. According to a 2013 cultural resources survey by the LCRA, the house started as a one-room cabin "sometime around 1900." The core wood cabin is a front-gabled single room with balloon-frame walls, board-and-batten vertical cladding, and a centrally located fireplace. There have been at least three recognizable sequences of improvements, including extra rooms, a screened back porch, an open front porch, and a carport for a total of 1,216 square feet of improvements. Historic outbuildings have included a possible outdoor

Historic Homestead: An early 1900s board-and-batten wood structure in the Uplands. Photo by Westcave staff

kitchen (close to a limestone barbecue pit), a hog pen, and an outhouse. The nearby field is now a prairie restoration project but had been used to grow both cotton and corn. Occupants or occasional visitors have included tenant farmers (see "A Copperhead and a Grave" in chapter 12) and land-owners, including the Chester Lay family (see "The Lay Ranch" in chapter 12), who owned the land from 1937 to 1966.

Native Prairie

During the spring and fall, the native prairie blooms into a painted land-scape of wildflowers that transforms into a sea of tall grasses in the drier seasons. In partnership with the US Fish and Wildlife Service, approximately eight acres bounded by the Prairie Loop are being restored to a native grass forb prairie. Nonnative and invasive plant species have been controlled through prescribed fire management, and native grasses and forbs have been reseeded or reintroduced. Visitors will see the mix of grasses that were present before humans used the land to graze livestock and grow crops. Restoring the prairie has helped to enrich the soil, increase biodiversity, prevent erosion, and attract more pollinators such as butterflies and hummingbirds. It also has provided important habitat for migratory birds and helped to control native but invasive woody plants such as Honey Mesquite, Ashe Juniper, and Poverty Weed.

Rest on one of several benches and enjoy the solitude, sounds of nature, and uncluttered views of the Hill Country. Spot the bat box or the bird traffic at the owl, Purple Martin, and bluebird boxes, or just pause and reflect, enjoy the shade and breeze, and imagine what the native animals are up to or what life was like for those who lived here long ago.

Picnic Area

Visitors are invited to use the picnic tables located south of the ELC near the solar array. Nearby, the pond stays filled year-round with captured rainwater, providing the local wildlife a refreshing drink and supporting a variety of plants and aquatic life. Look for open freshwater clam shells on the stonework, evidence of a raccoon who has eaten a meal in that spot.

4 ❧ EDUCATIONAL PROGRAMS AND ACTIVITIES

Westcave Outdoor Discovery Center's mission is to inspire people to develop a lifelong practice of enjoying and protecting nature. Westcave does this through ongoing conservation efforts at its spectacular Westcave Preserve and through educational activities designed to engage educators, parents, and children throughout central Texas. These include a variety of programs conducted through the Children in Nature Collaborative of Austin (CiNCA), both on-site and elsewhere. Westcave Preserve serves as an outdoor classroom for visitors to explore, discover, and appreciate their natural surroundings, but Westcave has ventured outside the bounds of its preserve to find new ways of connecting youth with nature. Two examples of Westcave's expanded community partnerships with that goal in mind are El Ranchito Summer Camp and the CiNCA, both described below.

Westcave advocates that, if from an early age kids learn to feel comfortable in nature, have access to it, understand its importance, and have fun outdoors, then the natural world will become an essential part of their daily lives, both as kids and adults.

Westcave Preserve Programs

The preserve itself is still at the core of Westcave's programs and activities. Educational programs begun in 1976 honor this "Crown Jewel of the Texas Hill Country" by teaching others about its unique ecology and the geologic and hydrologic forces that resulted in its creation. Westcave welcomes a growing number of visitors—currently more than ten thousand each year—for school field trips, public tours, topical programs, nature study, and guided and self-led hikes on the upland and canyon trails.

School Field Trips
Field trips are available to area educators by reservation. Their primary educational goal is to enhance school science education by offering an extraor-

dinary nature experience while supporting state-mandated learning requirements. Approximately five thousand schoolchildren each year learn about nature as they hike through hundreds of thousands of years of geological formations, watch the interface between groundwater and surface water at the spring-fed waterfall, and observe the changes in plant and animal life as they journey from the drier Uplands into the cooler, sheltered riparian canyon. All field trips are led by dedicated staff and designed for the specific grade level of the visiting class, and they can be tailored to the science concepts that are currently being taught in the classrooms.

On the John Covert Watson Canyon Trail, the 125 steps follow a natural crack in the Cow Creek limestone from the Uplands to the canyon floor sixty feet below. Photo by Ron Sprouse

Schools select from a variety of field trip topics, including:

- The Westcave Story (for all ages). Students observe the plants, animals, hydrology, and geology of Westcave Preserve and learn the importance of resource conservation by seeing how the preserve has recovered from environmental damage resulting from overuse prior to establishment of the preserve.
- Animals and Botanical Marvels (for all ages). In this program students learn about the wildlife, plants, and distinct habitats within the preserve and investigate biodiversity by conducting a biological survey.
- Water: Lifeblood of the Earth (for students in third grade and older). This activity examines the properties of water, our most precious resource. Students learn about the hydrologic (water) cycle, groundwater and aquifers, non-point source pollution, and rainwater harvesting.

A tour stops on the viewing deck. John Ahrns is in a white shirt, on the right. Photo by Westcave Staff

Westcave's educational programs begin before the students arrive at the preserve and linger beyond the bus ride home by providing curricula and materials for use in the classroom and on school grounds. Schoolchildren in the Austin, Dripping Springs, Eanes, Hays Consolidated, Johnson City, Lake Travis, Leander, Marble Falls, and Round Rock school districts are frequent visitors. Westcave charges a modest fee for these services but offers reduced-rate programs for schools that have a high percentage of students from low-income families.

Weekend Programs

Westcave Preserve offers a wide array of weekend programs for visitors of all ages. To protect the preserve's sensitive environment, entry into the canyon is available only through guided tours, offered every Saturday and Sunday (weather permitting) at 10 am, 12 noon, 2 pm, and 4 pm. The preserve also offers special programs throughout the year, including star parties, Golden-cheeked Warbler walks in the spring, and the annual Christmas Bird Count. All programs are listed online at www.westcave.org.

El Ranchito Summer Camp

El Ranchito Summer Camp began in 2007 as a collaboration among the Shield Ranch, El Buen Samaritano Episcopal Mission, and Westcave Preserve and was born out of a shared belief that it is important to provide urban kids with opportunities to discover the natural world—and themselves. In 2009 El Ranchito became a separate nonprofit organization as a project of the Shield Ranch Foundation, with Westcave Preserve and El Buen Samaritano continuing as primary collaborators. Westcave supports El Ranchito through nature curriculum and program planning, leading various staff training and camper programs, and hosting field trips.

The El Ranchito experience is designed to foster and nurture a sense of place, in which children—many for the first time—experience the land, its plants and animals, its streams, and the starry night sky, as well as sleeping in tents and eating outdoors. The camp philosophy includes a take-home approach, showing young people how to use their new skills, nature discoveries, and camp activities in their own neighborhoods and communities.

El Ranchito serves fourth through twelfth graders from low-income families and enjoys a 60 percent return rate each year. Camp sessions are kept small, and programs focus on fun nature exploration, conserva-

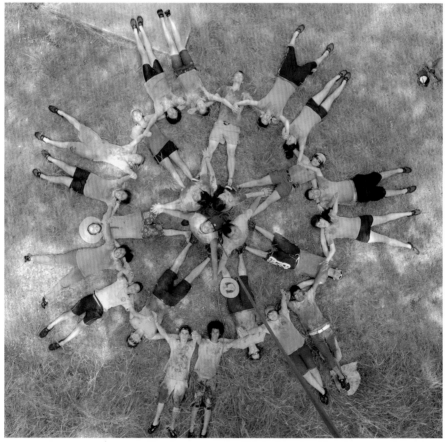

El Ranchito campers (in yellow shirts) and staff (in green shirts) in a meadow on the Shield Ranch near Westcave Preserve. Photo by Chris Keller

tion, and building camp communities that celebrate diversity and support every camper and staff member. Many of the campers attend this nature-immersion camp for five years or more, and some join the El Ranchito staff through a junior counselor program. In addition to the summer camp sessions and in response to parents' requests, El Ranchito offers family camp-outs to nearby state parks.

Learn about El Ranchito by visiting the website at www.elranchito.org.

Children in Nature Collaborative of Austin (CiNCA)

When Molly Stevens became Westcave's Preserve executive director in 2005, one of her first acts was to convene two dozen leaders with a connection to the preserve to envision the organization's next decade. To thank them, each was given a copy of *Last Child in the Woods, Saving our Children from Nature-Deficit Disorder*, by Richard Louv. This book reinforced the commitment of the preserve's board of directors to the deeper importance of reconnecting children to nature.

In 2009 Westcave Preserve launched CiNCA with a mission to ignite and fan the flames of the national movement to reconnect kids to the wonder and joy of the natural world and to inspire the next generation of environmental stewards. To achieve this goal, CiNCA unites schools, service providers, health care professionals, state and local government officials, and members of the community with a stake in developing children who are happier and healthier and who perform better in school as a result of

Children in the grotto area near the waterfall. Photo by Heather Kuhlken

being connected to nature on a regular basis. In 2012 the board of directors unanimously voted to incorporate CiNCA as a core program, and CiNCA has become a national model for collaboration among environmental non-profits. In 2013, Westcave announced the new name Westcave Outdoor Discovery Center to better represent the organization's range of programs, including its preserve and new Uplands property, its partnership role with El Ranchito Summer Camp, and its leadership of CiNCA.

The following are examples of CiNCA programs:

- The Roadrunner Outdoor Adventure Bus eliminates one of the greatest barriers schools and organizations face when attempting to offer outdoor environmental education experiences: expensive transportation. The bus is used by Westcave and other CiNCA members to take students on school field trips and to after-school and summer programs associated with the outdoors.
- The Natural Leaders Network of Austin works with youth and young adults between the ages of sixteen and twenty-nine who are interested in becoming leaders in environmental education, conservation, and outdoor recreation. This program includes quarterly conservation service projects, a five-day regional Legacy Camp, and green jobs networking opportunities through casual meet-ups and career fairs.
- The Green Schools Initiative supports tactical collaboration, resource sharing, and networking among area schools and regional organizations dedicated to environmental sustainability and also provides direct support to educators with resources and guidance.
- The Partnership for Childhood Wellness is a social change campaign for the families, neighborhoods, and schools in Austin where children's health is at greatest risk due to obesity. The Partnership leverages the combined influence of families, educators, health professionals, the faith community, and community developers to get kids outside and playing in nature as a way of combating unhealthy lifestyles.
- The Families and Community Task Force focuses on initiatives to engage parents and community leaders in efforts to get kids outside more often, with emphasis on acquainting families with the local nature community. Examples include Families in Nature, a nonprofit organization that encourages families to spend time together in the outdoors and to organize and launch their own family nature clubs. CiNCA also supports the Texas Nature Challenge and participation in Texas Parks and Wildlife Department's Texas Outdoor Families program.

PART 2
The Place

Rio Grande Leopard Frog (*Lithobates berlandieri*) making its escape. Illustration by Nancy McGowan

5 ❧ ENVIRONMENTAL SETTING

For sunny beauty of scenery and luxuriance of soil, it stands quite
unsurpassed in my experience, and I believe no region of equal
extent in the world can show equal attractions.

—Frederick Law Olmsted, *A Journey through Texas: Or a Saddle-Trip on
the Southwestern Frontier* (1857), *describing part of the Colorado River
watershed near Austin*

The environmental factors that characterize Westcave Preserve reflect
regional and local topography, geology, groundwater, surface water, climate, and, over the past fourteen thousand years, increasing human influences. Each of these factors affects the animal and plant life of the region
and influences the variety and quality of available habitats. The great diversity of fauna and flora at the preserve indicates that the environmental setting is particularly favorable.

The hilly terrain and canyonlands in the vicinity of the preserve have a
character that is different from the broad, flat to rolling upland landscape,
with few rivers, typical of the Edwards Plateau. In this part of the plateau,
also known as the Hill Country or the Balcones Canyonlands, rivers and
streams have dissected the land, forming a series of ridges separated by
deep, narrow valleys. Beds of Lower Cretaceous limestone and sandstone
underlie the plateau, and some of these rock layers are aquifers containing large volumes of groundwater. As the streams eroded into the plateau,
the aquifers were exposed and discharged through springs and seeps. The
emergent groundwater supplemented the volume of stream flow from runoff. As a result, perennial streams and rivers exist in this semiarid to subhumid climatic region, where rainfall is often so unreliable that most streams
would remain dry during parts of the year were it not for the contributions
from spring flow.

Rivers and streams have specific watersheds, which are topographic
basins that capture and direct the flow of runoff from rains and, in cold

climates, from snowmelt as well. Watersheds exist at all scales. Those of major rivers may encompass tens of thousands of square miles and the sub-sidiary watersheds of hundreds of smaller streams. The watershed of Heinz Branch is a component of the Pedernales River watershed, which in turn is a subdivision of the watershed of the Colorado River. From its headwaters in New Mexico, the Colorado flows generally southeastward into the Gulf of Mexico, adding contributions from each of its tributaries along the way. A small part of the water reaching the Gulf originated in the Heinz Branch watershed.

The Pedernales drainage is known for its steep canyon slopes, narrow drainage divides, and small valley floors, all of which contribute to the area's propensity for flash flooding.

Plants and Animals

Environmental conditions at Westcave Preserve support a particularly diverse flora and fauna. Over thousands of years, plants and animals have

The Uplands near the Historic Homestead, looking generally eastward. Photo by Molly Stevens

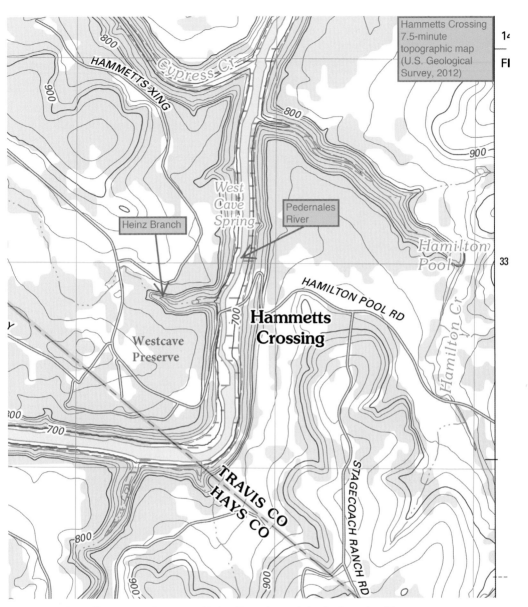

Location of Westcave Preserve, Heinz Branch, and the Pedernales River near Hammetts Crossing. Map by US Geological Survey

adapted to these conditions, which are different from those in other parts of the state but combine elements of each. The preserve lies at the intersection of several ecological provinces, each with its own assemblage of species. The ranges of these species overlap to a degree, enriching the local biotic composition. Species generally found in humid eastern regions thrive

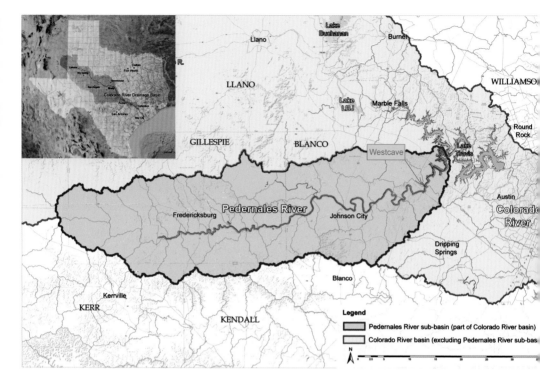

Westcave Preserve lies within the watershed of the Pedernales River, which flows into the Colorado River and southeast to the Gulf of Mexico. Map by J. Robert Anderson and Zixu Qiao

in the preserve's canyon and along the canyon rim, where spring discharge maintains an island of moisture. Among them, for example, are Spicebush and the Spicebush Swallowtail, Post Oak, Ruby-throated Hummingbird, and Bell's Vireo. Those species that prefer a comparatively dry climate, typical of the western part of the state, are quite at home in the Uplands, including Twisted-leaf Yucca and the Yucca Moth, Shin Oak, Black-chinned Hummingbird, and White-eyed Vireo. Other species, notably the many migratory birds, exhibit marked seasonal tolerances. Seasons are particularly important at Westcave and are discussed at length in chapter 6. For complete lists of species found or most likely to be found at Westcave Preserve, see the appendixes.

6 ❧ WESTCAVE PRESERVE THROUGH FOUR SEASONS

There were many flowers, that afternoon, on hills which a month ago were bleak as indigence. Recent rains followed by warm weather had coaxed out the tardiest buds, bringing to a climax a varicolored harvest of vast extent. Flowers were everywhere.

—Roy Bedichek, *Adventures with a Texas Naturalist* (1947, 1975)

It is often said, with some justification, that much of Texas has only two seasons: summer and almost summer. In central Texas, summer heat and humidity can be oppressive and unrelenting. Heat indexes and thermometer temperatures regularly reach 100°F, occasionally 110, with nighttime lows in the 70s and 80s. These conditions can be expected from July through August, or even from May through September. Hot, dry summers are the norm.

Yet despite the adage about two seasons only, weather in central Texas does vary through the year. Residents are almost as likely to complain about winter cold as they are about summer heat. Most of the records cited here are from weather stations located twenty to thirty miles to the east in Austin during the period of record, which began in 1897 (see chapter 10, "Climate and Weather," for detailed weather records). Temperatures in Austin have dropped as low as -5°F, but the winters are usually mild, with readings of freezing or below recorded on 19 to 25 days per year, depending on location.

Precipitation is distributed fairly evenly throughout the year, with totals peaking in May and September or October and falling in July or August. Nonetheless, flood-producing rains have been recorded in every month, and nearly every month has received no rain (≤0.1 inch) during at least one year. The heaviest rainfall events are associated with cold fronts in spring and with tropical hurricanes moving inland from the Gulf of Mexico or, less often, the Pacific Ocean, in summer and autumn. Weather extremes are part

A Note about Seasons

The existence of separate seasons of the year is one of nature's wonders. The world's temperate zones, between approximately 23.5 and 66.5 degrees latitude both north and south of the Equator and from sea level to approximately eleven thousand feet in elevation, are characterized by distinct seasonality, dividing the year into four periods of three months each: spring, from March through May; summer, from June through August; autumn, from September through November; and winter, from December through February. These are called the meteorological seasons, and described this way each is characterized by a particular temperature and precipitation regime, although the actual conditions are highly variable from year to year. The causes of seasonal and annual climatic differences are complex (see chapter 10, "Climate and Weather").

There also are astronomical seasons, which are similar but not identical to the seasons defined on a meteorological basis. Although astronomical seasons likewise divide the year into four equal parts, their divisions are based on changes in the alignment of Earth with respect to the Sun, rather than climate. Earth's axis of daily rotation is inclined approximately 23.5 degrees from perpendicular, relative to the plane of its annual orbit around the Sun. Because of this inclination, the amounts of solar radiation received by the Northern and Southern Hemispheres vary, as each is tilted either toward or away from the Sun at different points along the path of Earth's orbit. The time required to complete both an orbit of the Sun and the full range of hemispheric illumination is one year.

When the Northern Hemisphere faces the Sun most directly, it receives sunlight for a longer period each day than does the Southern Hemisphere, which is tilted away. The change in alignment is incremental, and for this reason the lengths of daylight and dark intervals change by only a few minutes per calendar day at any specific location on Earth's surface.

Twice during the annual orbit, the lengths of the daylight and dark periods are equal. These are the equinoxes, which occur on or about September 23 and March 21, varying by a day or two from year to year. The date of the shortest period of daylight in the Northern Hemisphere is the winter solstice, around December 22. The date of the longest period of daylight is the summer solstice, about June 21. Intervals between these benchmark dates are the astronomical seasons, and although their beginning and end dates differ from those of the meteorological seasons, the inclination of Earth's axis of rotation is the primary cause of both. Without this inclination, Earth would experience neither astronomical nor meteorological seasons.

Variation in the periods of daylight and seasonal light intensity drives Earth's weather systems, just as the changing seasons govern the lives of plants and animals.

of the local climate, but our environment is primarily regulated by the normal succession of hot-cold, wet-dry conditions.

In short, central Texas does, in fact, have four well-defined seasons.

Spring

At Westcave Preserve, as throughout the Northern Hemisphere Temperate Zone, spring is the time of renewal, when the warming land and waters awaken the flora and fauna from what was for many species winter's rest. Daytime temperatures are generally mild and nights are cool. In Austin, the average final date when temperatures fall to or below 32°F varies across the city from February 23 to March 4. The preserve is a few hundred feet higher

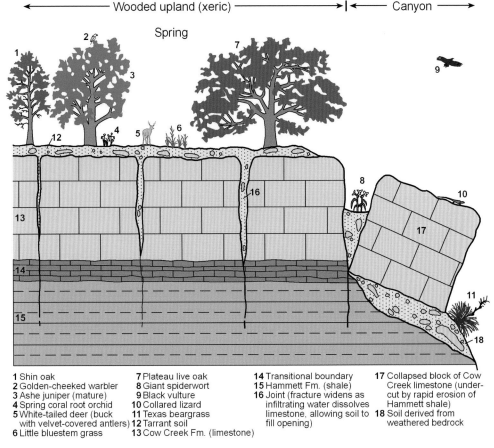

| ← Wooded upland (xeric) → | ← Canyon → |

1 Shin oak	7 Plateau live oak	14 Transitional boundary	17 Collapsed block of Cow
2 Golden-cheeked warbler	8 Giant spiderwort	15 Hammett Fm. (shale)	Creek limestone (under-
3 Ashe juniper (mature)	9 Black vulture	16 Joint (fracture widens as	cut by rapid erosion of
4 Spring coral root orchid	10 Collared lizard	infiltrating water dissolves	Hammett shale)
5 White-tailed deer (buck	11 Texas beargrass	limestone, allowing soil to	18 Soil derived from
with velvet-covered antlers)	12 Tarrant soil	fill opening)	weathered bedrock
6 Little bluestem grass	13 Cow Creek Fm. (limestone)		

Upland and canyon slope habitats, with representative fauna and flora (in spring).
Illustration by S. Christopher Caran and Joel Lardon

in elevation and much less influenced by urban heat sources, so it is likely that frosts there may linger to a later date.

During early spring northerly winds push cold fronts through intermittently, lowering temperatures for a few days, but within weeks the dominant wind direction gradually shifts to southerly, conveying both warm air from lower latitudes and moisture from the Gulf. This change, and the lengthening period of daylight, produces an overall rise in air temperature and atmospheric instability, enhancing the amount and frequency of rainfall. Cold fronts also may trigger spring thunderstorms, some of which are violent. Mean monthly precipitation increases from 1.7 inches in March to 4.2 inches in May, which, on average, is the year's wettest month.

Spring Flora

In response, large deciduous trees such as Bald Cypress, American and Cedar Elms, Sycamore, and Texas Oak produce leaf buds, then full canopies, early in spring, whereas more conservative species, particularly Pecan and Honey Mesquite, may delay leaf production well into April or May. By then, many trees, shrubs, and vines are in full flower, and a few, like the Red Mulberry, have produced copious fruit. The new leaves, flowers, and berries are nutritious, attracting wildlife of many kinds.

The Hill Country is famous for its wildflowers, which appear month-by-month according to a genetically predetermined, almost mystical timetable. Before you see them you might detect the sweet fragrance of the yellow flowers of Agarita, Texas Barberry, and Prickly Pear and the white blossoms of the Mexican Plum. The grape juice scent of the Mountain Laurel is as strikingly intense as the deep purple color of its large clusters of flowers.

Early spring is the time when the iconic Texas Bluebonnet may cover the landscape in swaths of blue and white. In contrast, the green-flowered Antelope Horns milkweed may bloom from spring through autumn. Giant Spiderworts produce flowers that range from lavender to pink amid the fractured gray limestone on the canyon's rim, where you also may see the spectacular pink blossoms of the Lace Cactus. In the canyon, giant Chatterbox Orchids bloom along the stream, and Missouri Violets, Columbines, and Inland Sea Oats are in flower among boulders beneath the canyon walls. If you are lucky, you might see the unusual blossoms of the Green Dragon. Other herbaceous plants also emerge, sprouting from roots or seeds or sending out shoots from a whorl of small leaves that have endured winter by hugging the ground for warmth and moisture.

Columbine (*Aquilegia canadensis*) in flower in Heinz Branch canyon. Common names include Red Columbine and Wild Columbine. Photo by Addie Louise Broussard

Rare Chatterbox Orchid (*Epipactis gigantea*) in flower in Heinz Branch canyon. Photo by Addie Louise Broussard

Inland Sea Oats (*Chasmanthium latifolium*) in flower. Illustration by Nancy McGowan

Rare Green Dragon (*Arisaema dracontium*) in flower in Heinz Branch canyon amist Virginia Creeper (*Parthenocissus quinquefolia*). Photo by Ron Sprouse

Spring Fauna
The rush of spring brings a return of migratory birds, including the Chimney Swift, Painted Bunting and Indigo Bunting, Summer Tanager, Eastern Wood-pewee, Black-chinned Hummingbird, Scissor-tailed Flycatcher, Northern Parula, White-eyed Vireo, and endangered Golden-cheeked Warbler, all intent on breeding and raising young.

Exhibiting traits of both Northern Parula (*Setophaga americana*) and Tropical Parula (*Setophaga pitiayumi*), this bird, possibly a hybrid, nests primarily in hanging Spanish Moss (*Tillandsia usneoides*). Photo by Arman Moreno

Golden-cheeked Warblers build their nests with the bark of mature Ashe Junipers and are so dependent on this resource that their nesting area precisely coincides with the central Texas range of these trees. Westcave Preserve contains an old-growth woodland of junipers that is regularly visited by the warbler, which nests within the preserve. Migratory Cedar Waxwings do not nest locally but often gather in large numbers to feed before heading north.

Many of our overwintering birds breed and brood here, including Cooper's Hawk, Eastern Screech-owl, Great Horned Owl, Black Vulture, Downy Woodpecker, Eastern Phoebe, and Canyon Wren. The owls are active at night and may be most easily recognized by their calls. By day, Lesser Goldfinches congregate in groups known as charms. You might see a squadron of American White Pelicans, a flotilla of Franklin's Gulls, or a kettle of Broad-winged and Swainson's Hawks, dozens to hundreds at a time, coming or going. The Mississippi Kite and Osprey are on the move as well, but prefer to travel alone.

Spring mammals, reptiles, amphibians, insects, and other invertebrates are also in reproductive mode. Virginia Opossum, Ringtail, Common Raccoon, Striped Skunk and Hog-nosed Skunk, Eastern Cottontail, Black-tailed Jackrabbit, Rock Squirrel, and Coyote produce their litters and watch over their young. White-tailed Deer, which breed year-round in suburban neighborhoods, are more likely to have their fawns in spring in more

Endangered Golden-cheeked Warbler

The Golden-cheeked Warbler (*Setophaga chrysoparia*) is a small migratory songbird that arrives at Westcave Preserve every March and April. The United States Fish and Wildlife Service, Texas Parks and Wildlife Department, and international agencies and organizations formally recognized the endangered status of this warbler in 1990. Its reduced numbers are primarily a result of the loss, fragmentation, and degradation of the bird's habitats both in central Texas and in its wintering grounds in Mexico and Central America. Nest parasitism by the Brown-headed Cowbird is another threat faced by this dazzling warbler, which weighs about 0.34 ounces (10 grams) and is about 4.7 inches (12 centimeters) long.

The male warblers are particularly colorful, with bright yellow cheeks and black throat and eye stripe. The males can be heard singing a variety of sweet, buzzy songs. Females are similar in appearance but are less bold in color. Golden-cheeks are insectivores, consuming a variety of insects, spiders, and caterpillars they glean in the oak-juniper woodlands. The arrival of the warbler each year is timed perfectly with a seasonal explosion of insects.

The warbler migrates each spring from Mexico, Honduras, Nicaragua, and Guatemala to breeding grounds exclusively in central Texas, where it usually remains through the summer, raising young. It requires mature Ashe Juniper bark to build its small, cuplike nest high in the canopies of oak, elm, or juniper, often near or on canyon edges or slopes. This ideal but dwindling habitat can be observed at Westcave Preserve and other areas of the Texas Hill Country.

Much of the habitat needed by the Golden-cheeked Warbler is part of the Balcones Canyonlands Preserve (BCP), a successful Hill Country effort that balances the protection of endangered species such as the Golden-cheeked with economic development. The BCP comprises over 30,500 acres scattered throughout western Travis County and is collectively managed in a public-private partnership.

Endangered Golden-cheeked Warbler (male).
Photo © Melody Lytle 2015

natural settings like Westcave Preserve.

As the air warms, Eastern Collared Lizard, Plateau Earless Lizard, Short-lined Skink, Texas Alligator Lizard, Great Plains Rat Snake, and Eastern Hog-nosed Snake are roused from the leaf litter, hollow logs, and rocky crevices that were their winter dens. The same is true in the Heinz Branch canyon and along the Pedernales River, where Blotched Water Snake, Redstriped Ribbon Snake, Red-eared Slider, and Guadalupe Spiny Softshell Turtle seem to materialize from the stones and logs on which they bask.

Ringtail (*Bassariscus astutus*) on Cow Creek limestone, with Giant Spiderwort (*Tradescantia gigantea*). Illustration by Nancy McGowan

Amphibians, too, appear as if by magic: Cliff Chirping Frog, Cope's Gray Treefrog, Green Treefrog, Woodhouse's Toad, and Rio Grande Leopard Frog announce their coming with sweet chanting. Some of these species are active only or primarily at night, but others by day when the weather is favorable. All are spring and summer breeders and can be found near water at those times. The Cliff Chirping Frog may occasionally be seen or heard in the cave and recesses in the canyon walls.

With the advance of spring, Riffle Beetles, caddisfly larvae, crayfish, and snails of the genus *Physella* become increasingly industrious.

Spring and early summer also are times when many butterflies and moths are at their busiest. Red Admirals, Question Marks, Spicebush Swallowtails, and Falcate Orangetips are especially prominent. The Red

Twisted-leaf Yucca and Yucca Moth

It is the most wonderful case of fertilisation [sic] ever published.
—Charles Darwin, letter to J. D. Hooker (1874)

The aptly named Yucca Moth is attracted to the fragrant flowers of the Twisted-leaf Yucca, a plant native to the Hill Country and common in Westcave Preserve's Uplands. The moth and plant perform an ecological duet known as obligate mutualism, in which one cannot survive without the other.

The female Yucca Moth enters the flower of the yucca at night, feeding on nectar and collecting pollen with a specialized mouth part. She punctures the flower's pistil with her ovipositor, inserts one or more eggs, then crawls to the opening of the stigma and inserts the pollen from that and other flowers she had entered previously. The pollen fertilizes the flower, thereby ensuring production of seeds. The yucca has no other means of pollination, as its flowers have an internal configuration that makes self-fertilization and pollen transfer from other insects unlikely. The stigma remains open only one or two nights, so pollination must occur then or not at all.

After an egg hatches, the larva remains well protected within the fleshy flower. The larva feeds only on newly formed yucca seeds, eating a few of those produced by each flower. When it has reached full size, the larva crawls out of the flower, falls to the ground, digs into the soil, and forms a chrysalis, from which an adult emerges in spring. The uneaten seeds are enclosed in a pod that forms shortly after the larvae leave the flower.

Clearly, each species is wholly and exclusively dependent on and beneficial to the other.

Female Yucca Moth (*Tegeticula yuccasella*) and Twisted-leaf Yucca (*Yucca rupicola*). Illustration by Brian Maebius. Photo © Steven Schwartzman

Admiral overwinters as an adult, not as a pupa. It is almost never seen until spring, then suddenly becomes abundant.

A different tactic is employed by a small moth that is perhaps equally common but remains inconspicuous. This is the aptly named Yucca Moth, with white forewings and white-fringed, predominantly gray hind wings. The female is attracted to the fragrant flowers of the Twisted-leaf Yucca, a plant endemic to the Hill Country and most of the Edwards Plateau and common in the preserve's Uplands. The moth and plant perform an ecological duet known as obligate mutualism, in which one cannot survive without the other (see the sidebar "Twisted-leaf Yucca and Yucca Moth").

Aquatic habitats of Heinz Branch and the contiguous Pedernales River support a diverse fauna that quickens in spring. Upstream from the waterfall, Heinz Branch is intermittent, and aquatic species are seen only after heavy rainstorms when the channel fills with runoff and overflow from livestock ponds in the upper part of the drainage basin. Conversely, fish and many invertebrates live year-round in the deep plunge pool beneath the waterfall and in the stream flowing from it. Some fish, including the Central Stoneroller (see the sidebar "Central Stoneroller"), Gray Redhorse, and Green Sunfish are moved by instinct to leave the pool or the adjacent Pedernales River and enter the swift shallows of the stream.

The Pedernales River is characterized by two distinct faunas. When the river is flowing normally, the fauna is similar to that of other perennial streams and rivers of the Hill Country and includes Red Shiners and Blacktail Shiners, Bluegill, Redear Sunfish, and Texas Logperch, among others. At times, however, the lower Pedernales River, including the reach near the preserve, is inundated by Lake Travis, a large artificial reservoir on the Colorado River that receives the Pedernales drainage. When Lake Travis rises above 681 feet, lake water extends upstream as much as several miles into the Pedernales valley. During these periods, which sometimes last several months, the aquatic fauna of the flowing river is joined by lake dwellers such as Longnose Gar, Gizzard Shad, River Carpsucker, and Flathead Catfish.

Summer

In summer, a slower, steady pace replaces the exuberant abundance of spring. Temperatures climb steadily, and although June often affords a comfortable transition, the days of hot, humid weather can sometimes begin early and forge an unbroken chain lasting through August. If there

Central Stoneroller

In spring the Central Stoneroller, a small member of the minnow family, moves through the swift shallows of the canyon's stream. When making its way upstream, the stoneroller is capable of climbing nearly vertical sections of a stream bed, using its pectoral fins and tail to crawl and swim through just a thin film of water. The male typically selects a site that is close to the preserve's plunge pool, then excavates and defends a nest on the channel floor. The clear, riffling stream waters are ideal for the stoneroller, which, true to its name, often moves stones to build a suitable nest. After the female lays eggs within the nest, the male fertilizes and covers them and remains nearby to protect them.

What sets this endeavor apart from those of other fish species at Westcave Preserve is that the nests are maintained in the midst of human presence. Visitors regularly are in close proximity to the occupied nests while crossing the stream near the grotto.

Male Central Stoneroller (*Campostoma anomalum*) in stream riffle. Illustration by Nancy McGowan

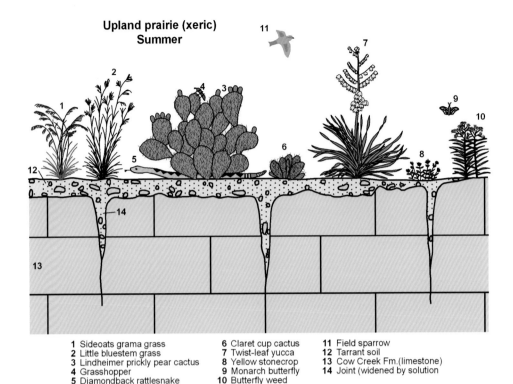

Upland prairie (xeric)
Summer

1 Sideoats grama grass	6 Claret cup cactus	11 Field sparrow
2 Little bluestem grass	7 Twist-leaf yucca	12 Tarrant soil
3 Lindheimer prickly pear cactus	8 Yellow stonecrop	13 Cow Creek Fm.(limestone)
4 Grasshopper	9 Monarch butterfly	14 Joint (widened by solution
5 Diamondback rattlesnake	10 Butterfly weed	

The Uplands prairie habitat, with representative fauna and flora (in summer).
Illustration by S. Christopher Caran and Joel Lardon

is little rainfall, many organisms simply endure the summer months as best they can. Mean maximum daily temperatures increase to 96.1°F, while monthly precipitation drops to less than 2.0 inches—often, much less.

Summer Flora

The Uplands area at Westcave Preserve is unprotected from the sun and, during most of the year, has no immediate source of water other than rainfall. Plants must be capable of obtaining soil moisture at depth and resisting excessive evaporative losses. They also may need defenses against wholesale browsing and insect damage. The harsh seasonal conditions select for deep-rooted, drought-tolerant trees, shrubs, and cacti, which tend to have leaves that are spiny, coarse, unpalatable, or even poisonous or covered in short bristles or a waxy substance. Prickly Pear, Ashe Juniper, Agarita, Kidneywood, Twisted-leaf Yucca, Gum Elastic, and Scrub Live Oak are examples.

Velvetleaf Senna (*Senna lindheimeriana*) blooms from late summer into autumn.
Photo by Amber Ahrns Gosselin

Some plants that may appear unadapted to this environment are in fact able to survive and thrive, even in the open or in rocky recesses where they are sheltered from harsh sunlight and winds. Plants flowering in the Uplands during summer include Mexican Hat, Indian Blanket, Rose Mallow, and Velvet Mallow. Velvetleaf Senna produces large, golden blossoms from late summer into autumn.

In a terrain otherwise dominated by dry conditions, the moist canyon environment is an anomaly. The steep canyon walls are rimmed with trees that reduce the amount of direct sunlight reaching the canyon floor, and tall trees growing along the stream create deep shade. Water flowing through the canyon also moderates air temperatures. The cool groundwater coming from springs at the canyon's head and points along the walls maintains a temperature of around 68°F throughout the year and chills the air through direct contact and evaporation. The result is that air temperatures in the canyon can be as much as ten degrees cooler than those in the Uplands.

In summer droughts the flow of springwater over the waterfall may

Redbay (*Persea borbonia*) with fruit.
Illustration by Nancy McGowan

Lindheimer's Shieldfern (*Thelypteris ovata var. lindheimeri*) in Heinz Branch canyon. Photo by Ron Sprouse.

be reduced from effusive to meager, but it is enough, along with that of smaller springs emerging from the canyon walls further downstream, to maintain stream flow throughout the canyon. This habitat supports a diverse flora, even in the driest years, including a conifer and several hardwoods at or near the western edge of their ranges: Bald Cypress, Chinkapin Oak, Redbay, Spicebush, Rusty Blackhaw, Sycamore-leaf Snowbell, and Carolina Basswood. Horsetail, Lindheimer's Shieldfern, and Maidenhair Fern grow along the stream, and Mexican Flowering Fern, Alabama Lipfern, Powdery Cloakfern, and Purple Cliff Brake Fern grow in pores and fractures in the limestone canyon rocks and walls.

Some fruits ripen in summer, including those of Rusty Blackhaw, Texas Persimmon, Mexican Plum, and Mustang Grape late in the season. At these times Common Raccoons and Ringtails eat heartily, as do Northern Mockingbirds, Common Gray Foxes, and Coyotes. The Texas Prickly Pear produces a large edible fruit known as a tuna. Toward the end of summer, the tunas ripen to deep purple and are eaten by Wild Turkeys and many mammals, including Virginia Opossums, Rock Squirrels, Common Hognosed Skunks, and White-tailed Deer.

The red flowers of Turk's Cap are a favorite of hummingbirds, while Blue

Powdery Cloakfern (Agryrochosma dealbata) on Cow Creek limestone below the canyon rim. Photo by Addie Louise Broussard

Mistflowers attract many butterflies. Three vines with unusual flowers grow in the understory: Purple Leatherflower has a flower shaped like a vase; Pearl Milkweed Vine has a green flower with a raised, pearl-like structure in the center; and Yellow Passionflower has a small, and extremely complex yellow-green, flower.

Summer Fauna

Differences among the preserve's habitats are especially pronounced in summer, and some species commute daily from the Uplands to wetter habitats in the canyon or along the river. Many birds are at home in the Uplands in summer: Red-shouldered Hawk and Red-tailed Hawk,

Northern Bobwhite, Mourning Dove and Inca Dove, Greater Roadrunner, Western Kingbird, Scissor-tailed Flycatcher, Bewick's Wren, and Eastern Bluebird. These birds seem to find all they need in the dry savanna, where rodents, insects, grass seeds, berries, lizards, and snakes serve as food.

Most mammals remain hidden during the day, but the Nine-banded Armadillo, Black-tailed Jackrabbit, and Eastern Fox Squirrel are seen fairly often. Common Gray Fox, Eastern Cottontail, and Rock Squirrel may be observed at dawn and dusk, while at night Virginia Opossum, Striped Skunk, and, occasionally, Common Porcupine are especially active. Cave Myotis and Brazilian Free-tailed Bat join the Common Poorwill and Chuck-will's-widow in their nightly aerial pursuit of moths and other flying insects. On the ground, Texas Horned Lizard and Six-lined Race runner hunt Leafcutting Ants and Harvester Ants, primarily by day.

Purple Leatherflower (*Clematis pitcheri*) in flower. Illustration by Nancy McGowan

Yellow Passionflower (*Passiflora lutea*) in bloom. Photo by Addie Louise Broussard

Summer Fauna of the Canyon

Different animals are present in the canyon, including two of the most elusive birds in North America, which are more often heard than seen. The Yellow-billed Cuckoo feeds on caterpillars high in the trees, while the Least Bittern hunts for small fish and invertebrates in the stream near the canyon's mouth. Not so elusive is the Green Kingfisher, which also watches for fish such as the Red Shiner and Western Mosquitofish. Among the larger fishes found in the plunge pool and downstream, Bluegill and Longear Sunfishes and Yellow Bullhead breed in the shallows in early summer, sometimes attracting the attention of the Western Cottonmouth. All the while, Red Saddlebags Dragonflies and Common Whitetail Dragonflies patrol the edges of the pool and skim the water's surface to lay eggs.

Autumn

Autumn is another season of transition when nature distills the excesses of summer to a welcome softness. In some years temperatures drop dramati-

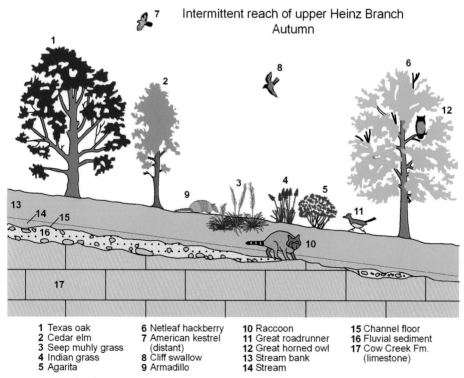

Intermittent reach of upper Heinz Branch
Autumn

1 Texas oak	6 Netleaf hackberry	10 Raccoon	15 Channel floor
2 Cedar elm	7 American kestrel	11 Great roadrunner	16 Fluvial sediment
3 Seep muhly grass	(distant)	12 Great horned owl	17 Cow Creek Fm.
4 Indian grass	8 Cliff swallow	13 Stream bank	(limestone)
5 Agarita	9 Armadillo	14 Stream	

Upper reach of Heinz Branch in the Uplands, with representative fauna and flora (in autumn). Illustration by S. Christopher Caran and Joel Lardon

cally, almost overnight, and rain chances rise just as quickly. Rainstorms are common during September and October and can produce floods. The Hill Country of central Texas is one of the most flood-prone areas in the continental United States. In autumn the cause is most often the intense rain from tropical storms and hurricanes.

Autumn Flora

Gentle, well-timed rains are, however, the hopeful choice. They bring a fresh surge of autumn wildflowers across the Uplands, particularly Tall Goldenrod, Gayfeather, Frostweed, and several asters and nightshades. The Purple Passionflower produces an edible fruit known as the maypop, which is eaten by mammals and birds alike. When conditions are favorable, Scrub Live Oak, Shin Oak, Post Oak, Texas Oak, and Chinkapin Oak become heavily laden with acorns, which are a year-round staple for White-tailed Deer, Turkeys, Rock Squirrels, and Eastern Fox Squirrels. Pecans are especially nutritious and are eaten and stored by both Western Scrubjays and squirrels. The fruits of Ashe Juniper, Prairie Flameleaf Sumac, Evergreen Sumac, Virginia Creeper, Poison Ivy, Texas Persimmon, Mustang Grape, and Elbow Bush are important food for numerous birds and mammals.

As the period of daylight shortens and the sunlight's intensity is diminished, air temperatures cool, and the leaves of deciduous trees blush into color. If the moisture and temperature conditions are right, including a brief period of frost, the foliage of deciduous trees will paint the hillsides and valleys. When at their most colorful, the leaves of some common trees turn as follows:

Bald Cypress (needles), golden brown
Chinkapin Oak, yellow-brown
Post Oak, orange or yellow
Texas Oak, shades of red and orange
Prairie Flameleaf Sumac, brilliant red
Rusty Blackhaw, orange-red to red and purple
Redbay, deep red
Redbud, greenish yellow, yellow, or orange
Cedar Elm, golden yellow and orange
Rough-leaf Dogwood, yellow-brown
Poison Ivy, orange or red
Mustang Grape, red with yellow along veins, then yellow

Autumn Fauna

To take advantage of autumn food sources, some birds, including Sandhill Cranes, Snow Geese, and many ducks, migrate through the Westcave Preserve area toward southern regions. Their musical calls to one another are the thrilling essence of all that is wild. There is also an ingress of Sharp-shinned Hawks and nonresident Cooper's Hawks, which may spend the winter. But Mississippi Kites and Swainson's and Broad-winged Hawks take flight for other climes, as do Little Blue Herons and Green Herons and many of the smaller shorebirds, nightjars, humming-birds, and warblers. Monarch butterflies continue their epic journey south, accompanied by Brazilian Free-tailed Bats, which are the only common mammals to leave the area in autumn.

Texas Oak (*Quercus buckleyi*) leaf in autumn. Scan by S. Christopher Caran

The aquatic habitats at the preserve remain relatively stable well into autumn, although floods may occasionally disrupt this environment. The first freeze occurs about November 27 on average. Much of the flow through the plunge pool and lower stream is supplied by groundwater at a nearly constant temperature, so the water bodies themselves do not freeze over. On cold days fish move out of the shallows into deeper water, and the turtles may disappear into burrows. Water snakes may still be seen on sunny days, but they and the turtles will eventually hibernate. Black-crowned Night-herons are active throughout the autumn and winter, always ready to prey on any small vertebrates or invertebrates.

Monarch butterfly (*Danaus plexippus*) on flowers of Orange Milkweed (*Asclepias tuberosa*). Photo by Heather Kuhlken

Winter

Throughout central Texas, winter is generally mild. Periods of subfreezing temperatures are usually measured in hours and may be dry. Periods of snow or ice are the most memorable winter events. Snow is uncommon, but ice may last for several days in the shaded canyon. Icicles as much as forty feet long have been seen to extend from the top of the waterfall to the surface of the plunge pool, although events of this type are rare. Ice also may coat the travertine deposits, mirroring their undulating surface.

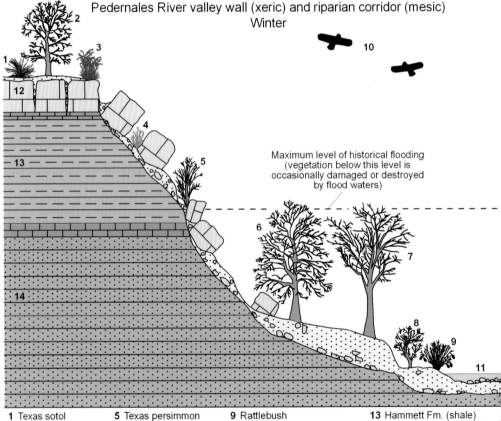

Pedernales River valley wall (xeric) and riparian corridor (mesic)
Winter

Maximum level of historical flooding
(vegetation below this level is
occasionally damaged or destroyed
by flood waters)

1 Texas sotol	5 Texas persimmon	9 Rattlebush	13 Hammett Fm. (shale)
2 Shin oak	6 Sycamore	10 Turkey vulture	14 Sycamore Fm. (sandstone)
3 Texs kidneywood	7 Bald cypress	11 Pedernales River channel	
4 Mormon tea	8 Black willow	12 Cow Creek Fm. (limestone)	

Pedernales River valley habitats—upland, canyon wall, river terrace, and channel—with representative fauna and flora (in winter). Illustration by S. Christopher Caran and Joel Lardon

Icicles adorn the Westcave waterfall. Photo by Addie Louise Broussard

In the canyon, all of the deciduous trees, including the Bald Cypress, are entirely bare, allowing sunlight to reach the canyon floor for the few hours each day when the Sun is high enough to shine into the canyon. An early frost may affect the aptly named Frostweed, a tall herb with an erect stem, causing the plant's sap to freeze and break through the stems, forming undulant bands of white, frothy ice. A surprising amount of ice may emerge, forming a low mound of ribbons around the plant.

Most plants are in repose throughout the winter, but not the evergreen Ashe Juniper. Male trees have numerous tiny cones containing large amounts of pollen. This is an unhappy season for those who suffer from the allergy known as cedar

Eastern Cottonwood (*Populus deltoides*), naturally skeletonized leaf (in winter). Scan by S. Christopher Caran

fever, but the pollen fertilizes female junipers, which produce an abundance of pea-sized berries eaten by wildlife.

Winter Fauna

Some wildlife remains active or at least visible, including the Western Scrub-jay and Common Raven as well as several species of sparrows, including Grasshopper, Fox, Song, Lincoln's, White-throated, Harris's, and White-crowned Sparrows. The American Woodcock occasionally occupies the canyon. Sharp-shinned, Cooper's, Red-shouldered, and Red-tailed Hawks and the Eastern Screech-owl and Great Horned Owl also linger through the winter.

Larger mammals continue their normal behavior, but when the weather is severe most seek shelter in a seasonal den or wherever cover is available. The Cave Myotis bat is probably the only mammal to truly hibernate. It sometimes occupies small holes in the ceiling of the cave, often where it can be seen by visitors.

Frostweed (*Verbesina virginica*). During freezing weather the stems secrete delicate white icy ribbons. Photo by Addie Louise Broussard

(BELOW) An American Woodcock (*Scolopax minor*), also known as the Timberdoodle, in Heinz Branch canyon, observed during a Christmas Bird Count. Photo by Arman Moreno

Red-eared Slider turtles (*Trachemys scripta elegans*) sunning on log. Illustration by Nancy McGowan

The Red Admiral and possibly other butterflies are known to overwinter at the preserve, although they are rarely observed until spring. Fish can be seen in the pool on most days, whereas the Red-eared Slider turtle and some water snakes are encountered only when the weather is warm.

Conclusion

You have completed your vicarious journey through the four seasons at Westcave Preserve. Did you wince at the keen edge of a "blue norther" cold front? Did the summer heat make you roll up your sleeves? This was only a glimpse, a postcard saying "wish you were here." The Westcave magic must be experienced firsthand in all the seasons. There are mysteries still unexplored.

This Cave Myotis bat (*Myotis velifer*) hibernated in the cave at the preserve from November 2014 to February 2015. Photo by Addie Louise Broussard

7 ❧ GEOLOGY

Topography and Ancient Bedrock

Westcave Preserve comprises several distinct topographic features:

- The cave, a partly enclosed, natural overhang and waterfall at the head of Heinz Branch canyon;
- The canyon itself, which is the lower reach of Heinz Branch, draining one-quarter mile eastward through a steep-walled canyon to the western bank of the Pedernales River;
- The steep canyon wall of the Pedernales River and the flat river terrace on its western bank; and
- The uplands plateau surrounding the rim of the Heinz Branch and Pedernales River canyons and part of the watershed and shallow channel of upper Heinz Branch, which is an intermittent stream.

Westcave Preserve's waterfall and cave are considered its main attractions. Located at the head of the Heinz Branch slot canyon, the waterfall drops forty feet into a natural pool below. In geomorphological terms, the waterfall is an example of a knickpoint—a place where the elevation and gradient of the stream channel change abruptly.

Another important geological feature—the cavelike enclosure that gives Westcave Preserve its name—is adjacent to the waterfall's plunge pool. It is not a typical cave but was formed by a massive accumulation of travertine draperies that walled off part of the overhang. The travertine is formed from seepage of springwater from the canyon rim.

There are a number of ancient bedrock types exposed at the preserve or nearby. Glen Rose, Hensell, Cow Creek, Hammett, and Sycamore strata were deposited during the Early Cretaceous Period, approximately 120 million to 100 million years ago. These formations are underlain by the Smithwick Formation, of Pennsylvanian age, which is more than 300 million years old and is not exposed within the preserve.

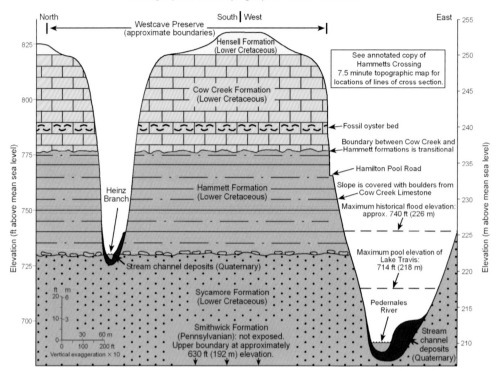

Stratigraphic and topographic cross-section

Westcave geology and topography. Illustration by S. Christopher Caran and Joel
Lardon

Glen Rose Formation: Stair-Stepped "Dinosaur Rock"

Hilltops in the upper part of the Heinz Branch watershed and on the eastern side of the Pedernales River within view from the preserve are capped by
the Glen Rose Formation, consisting of alternating thin beds of limestone
and marl (muddy limestone). Marl erodes more easily than limestone, and
as erosion removes the rock, layer by layer, the limestone beds are exposed
as broad, flat surfaces, whereas the more easily eroded marl forms steep
slopes protected beneath the next higher bed of limestone.

This pattern of erosion produces slopes with a stair-stepped appearance that is characteristic of the Glen Rose. Weathering of the exposed beds
yields a soil called the Brackett series. The Glen Rose Formation was named
for the town of Glen Rose, located southwest of Fort Worth. Dinosaur

Valley State Park near Glen Rose is the site of numerous dinosaur tracks, and tracks have been found in outcrops of the Glen Rose Formation near Westcave Preserve. The Glen Rose is more than six hundred feet thick, but in the preserve's immediate area erosion has stripped away all but a thin remnant, which overlies the Hensell Formation. The Glen Rose Formation is not present within the preserve.

Hensell Formation: Reddish Brown Soil Good for Growing Peaches

The Hensell Formation is a soft, clayey sandstone approximately eighty feet thick, but only about ten feet remains within the preserve. It can be found on the flat terrain upstream from the waterfall and canyon. The sandstone is deeply weathered to a reddish brown soil known as the Volente series.

Soil derived from this formation is also present in the Fredericksburg area in central Texas, where German farmers discovered that it was ideal for growing peaches. The sandstone is the namesake of the nearby Hensel Ranch, where the formation was first described but was misspelled. The spelling error persists to this day. At Westcave Preserve, erosion has removed most of the Hensell sandstone, exposing a hard, erosion-resistant yet porous limestone beneath.

Cow Creek Formation: A Durable, Porous Aquifer

The limestone beneath the Hensell Formation is known as the Cow Creek Formation. It is widely exposed within the preserve, where it forms the canyon rim and much of the uplands plateau. As the limestone weathers, it produces the thin Tarrant soil series.

The Cow Creek Formation is forty-five feet thick, and it was named for exposures along Cow Creek east of the Pedernales River. This highly durable limestone supports the waterfall at the head of the Heinz Branch Canyon and protects the grotto. It is also an important aquifer and provides the spring flow that maintains both the waterfall and the stream in dry weather.

At the base of the Cow Creek Formation are approximately ten feet of interbedded thin limestone and sandy mudstone beds. This transition zone separates the thick beds of honeycombed Cow Creek limestone from the underlying Hammett Formation, which is composed of relatively soft siltstone, sandstone, and shale. A fossil oyster bed in these strata can be seen in the roof and rear wall of the cave and behind the waterfall.

Hammett Formation

The Hammett Formation forms the lower part of the walls of Heinz Branch Canyon but is poorly exposed and is best observed beneath the overhang in the cave and grotto at the head of the canyon. This formation, sixty feet thick, takes its name from Hammetts Crossing, which is where the formation was originally defined. Hammetts Crossing was a historical ford on the lower Pedernales River immediately upstream from (south of) the mouth of Heinz Branch, where Hamilton Pool Road crosses the river today. Where the road rises from the low-water bridge on the western side of the river, the Hammett Formation can be seen in the road cut.

Sycamore Formation

The Sycamore Formation underlies the Hammett and is likewise exposed at Hammetts Crossing and the mouth of Heinz Branch. Named for outcrops along nearby Sycamore Creek, the Sycamore Formation is seventy-five feet thick in this area, although only the upper forty feet are exposed. The Sycamore Formation is composed of sandstone and conglomerate and contains thin beds of lignite, a form of coal. The Sycamore is the oldest stratum exposed in the Westcave Preserve area and forms the base of the sequence of rock formations that were deposited during the Cretaceous Period.

Smithwick Formation

The Sycamore overlies the Smithwick Formation, which was deposited during the Pennsylvanian age more than 300 million years ago. The Sycamore and Smithwick Formations are separated by a 180-million-year gap in the geological record of this region. The gap was caused by erosion of the rock strata that were deposited in the intervening time interval, prior to deposition of the Sycamore.

The Smithwick Formation was named for the community of Smithwick located nearby. In this area the total thickness of the sandstone and shale composing the Smithwick Formation is three hundred feet. At present, these strata are not exposed locally, but they lie at shallow depth beneath the channel deposits of the Pedernales River. From time to time flooding has eroded these channel gravels, exposing the Smithwick Formation briefly.

Table 7.1. Rocks and Soils of Westcave Preserve

Stratigraphic Unit	Maximum Thickness	General Composition	Physical Properties; Location and/or Outcrop
Quaternary Period (2.58 million years ago to the present) *Holocene Epoch (11,700 years ago to the present)*			
Soil: unconsolidated to moderately consolidated sediment; soil series not determined	3 to 10 feet	Sandy to clayey with cobbles and boulders	Loose, well drained; in and along channels of lower Heinz Branch and slopes below canyon rim, beneath overhang, and in cave
Soil: soil series not determined	~2 feet	Sandy to clayey, usually covered with boulders	Loose, well drained to moderately well drained; slopes below canyon rim on outcrops of Hammett Formation shale and sandstone
Soil: Tarrant series	<2 feet	Stony clay	Cohesive, well drained; uplands above canyon rim; on Cow Creek limestone
Soil: Volente series	~4 feet	Silty clay loam and clay loam	Cohesive, moderately well drained; uplands above canyon rim; on Hensell Formation clayey sandstone
Soil: Brackett series	2–4 feet	Gravelly clay loam to clay loam	Cohesive, well drained; uplands in upper Heinz Branch watershed on Glen Rose Formation limestone and marl
Travertine and speleothems	<1–10 feet	Calcareous mounds, draperies, stalactites, stalagmites	Hard to soft, laminated; head and walls of Heinz Branch canyon, beneath overhang, and in cave
Pleistocene Epoch (2.58 million years to 11,700 years ago)			
Travertine	3–6 feet	Calcareous mounds, draperies	Hard, laminated; Heinz Branch canyon walls (downstream)
Terrace deposits	3–35 feet	Sand and gravel, partly cemented with calcium carbonate	Loose to hard, porous; Heinz Branch and Pedernales River canyons beneath channels and along canyon walls
Early Cretaceous Period (120 to 100 million years ago)			
Glen Rose Formation	600 feet, thicker elsewhere (not present within Westcave Preserve)	Alternating thin beds of limestone and marl	Soft to moderately hard, slowly permeable; isolated hilltops in upper Heinz Branch watershed and on eastern side of Pedernales River
Hensell Formation	<6 feet locally, 80 feet regionally	Fine-grained sandstone	Soft, easily eroded, slowly permeable; isolated remnants in uplands above canyon rim

Stratigraphic Unit	Maximum Thickness	General Composition	Physical Properties; Location and/or Outcrop
Cow Creek Formation	45 feet (35 feet above transition zone)	Limestone: highly porous, fossiliferous, fractures locally	Hard, dense, stable, high load-bearing capacity, unstable where fractured along canyon rim, highly permeable; uplands and canyon rim
Basal Cow Creek Formation (Cow Creek–Hammett transition)	~10 feet	Interbedded limestone and sandy mudstone, fossiliferous	Soft, slowly permeable, mudstone beds weather recessively, thin limestone beds remain prominent; beneath thick limestone beds forming canyon rim
Hammett Formation	60 feet	Shale with thin beds of sandstone	Soft, weathered surface slakes, forming wide recess beneath overhang, relatively impermeable; almost entirely covered with travertine at head of canyon and with large fallen blocks of limestone along the canyon walls
Sycamore Formation	75 feet (only 40 feet exposed locally)	Calcareous sandstone and conglomerate	Hard, weathers to an irregular slope, permeable; banks of lower Heinz Branch and Pedernales River
Pennsylvanian Period (300 million years ago)			
Smithwick Formation	300 feet, not exposed locally	Shale with thin beds of sandstone	Generally soft with few hard beds, relatively impermeable; underlies Sycamore Formation throughout Westcave Preserve and surrounding area, but not exposed within the preserve; underlies channel deposits of Pedernales River at shallow depth

Table 7.2. Geological Time Scale

Phanerozoic Eon (541.0 Ma–present)	Cenozoic Era (66.0 Ma–present)	Quaternary Period (2.58 Ma–present)	Holocene Epoch (11,700 yr–present)
			Pleistocene Epoch (2.58 Ma–11,700 yr)
		Tertiary Period, Neogene Subperiod (23.0–2.58 Ma)	Pliocene Epoch (5.3–2.58 Ma)
			Miocene Epoch (23.0–5.3 Ma)
		Tertiary Period, Paleogene Subperiod (66.0–23.0 Ma)	Oligocene Epoch (33.9–23.0 Ma)
			Eocene Epoch (56.0–33.9 Ma)
			Paleocene Epoch (66.0–56.0 Ma)
	Mesozoic Era (252.2–66.0 Ma)	Cretaceous Period (145.0–66.0 Ma)	Late Cretaceous (100.5–66.0 Ma)
			Early Cretaceous (145.0–100.5 Ma)
		Jurassic Period (201.3–145.0 Ma)	NR
		Triassic Period (252.2–201.3 Ma)	NR
	Paleozoic Era (541.0–252.2 Ma)	Permian Period (298.9–252.2 Ma)	NR
		Pennsylvanian or Late Carboniferous Period (323.2–298.9 Ma)	NR
		Mississippian or Early Carboniferous Period (358.9–323.2 Ma)	NR
		Devonian Period (419.2–358.9 Ma)	NR

	Silurian Period (443.8–419.2 Ma)	NR	
	Ordovician Period (485.4–443.8 Ma)	NR	
	Cambrian Period (541.0-485.4 Ma)	NR	
Proterozoic Eon (2500–541.0 Ma)	NR	NR	NR
Archean Eon (~4000–2500 Ma)	NR	NR	NR
Hadean Eon (~4600–4000 Ma)	NR	NR	NR
	Origin of Earth: ~5500 Ma		

Source: The names and ages of these time intervals are consistent with the 2015 standards of the International Commission on Stratigraphy.

Notes: All ages are in years before the present.

Ma = million (10^6) years before the present

yr = years before the present

NR = Time division is not recognized or is not relevant to the present discussion. Numbers in parentheses denote ages of exposed bedrock and sedimentary deposits.

8 🌿 EVOLUTION OF WESTCAVE PRESERVE

250,000 Years Ago to the Present

At Westcave Preserve and throughout central Texas, the landscape has changed dramatically over the past 2.58 million years—the time interval known as the Quaternary Period. The precise timing of changes in the landscape is not well known, but it is probable that about 100,000 years ago Westcave Preserve's main geologic feature, the Heinz Branch slot canyon, was formed. Eroded materials have scraped Heinz Branch and other canyons and valleys ever deeper into the Hill Country landscape.

Recent investigations have provided evidence regarding geological events during the last 250,000 years. The following reconstruction of landscape evolution in the Westcave area is based on that evidence. The reconstruction also is detailed in four color panels on the outside east wall of the ELC.

Some 250,000 years ago, the amount of water flowing through the ancestral Pedernales River may have been greater than it is today. The river had a broad, shallow valley and channel. Low hills dotted a relatively flat upland landscape, which may have been covered with prairie grasses. The river flowed over ancient marine limestone and sandstone that was deposited much earlier, during part of the Early Cretaceous Period from approximately 120 million to 100 million years ago. Across most of the landscape, only the Glen Rose Formation was exposed.

The river gradually eroded entirely through the Glen Rose rock and into the underlying Hensell Formation. The soft Hensell sandstone eroded easily, allowing the river to cut ever deeper. Soon, the river reached the upper Cow Creek Formation, where further downcutting was impeded. The Cow Creek limestone is relatively thin but very hard. Instead of deepening its valley further, the river probably began to meander across the top of the Cow Creek Formation, eroding the much softer Hensell and Glen Rose Formations along its banks, thus creating a broad valley.

250,000 Years Ago

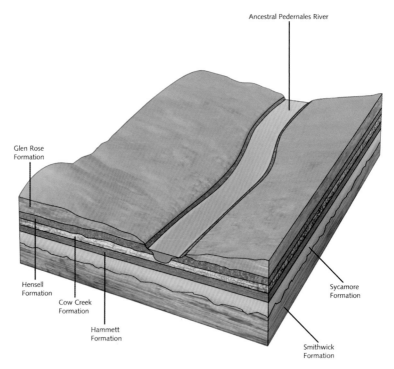

Westcave area landscape 250,000 years ago. The ancestral Pedernales River became entrenched. Illustration by S. Christopher Caran and Tim Hayes

Heinz Branch

In the area that became Heinz Branch Canyon, downward erosion was slowed by the Cow Creek rock, and the river may not have cut through these hard layers until approximately one hundred thousand years ago. In contrast, rain and runoff quickly eroded the walls of the ancestral Pedernales River valley. In this area, outcrops of the Glen Rose and Hensell Formations receded far from the river, leaving only remnants.

It was at about that time that Heinz Branch may have formed as a tiny tributary to the river, perhaps when severe floods scoured the river channel and undercut the mouth of the small stream that would become Heinz Branch. Other streams, including nearby Hamilton Creek, also may have had their origin at that time.

Eventually the river breached the Cow Creek Formation within its own

100,000 Years Ago

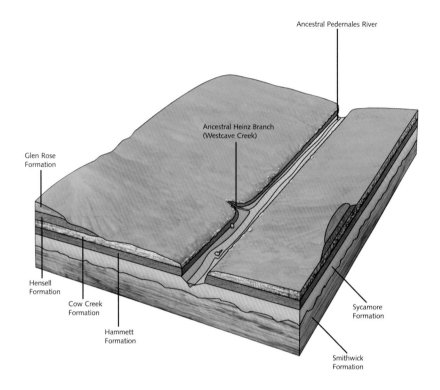

Ancestral Pedernales River

Ancestral Heinz Branch
(Westcave Creek)

Glen Rose
Formation

Hensell
Formation

Cow Creek
Formation

Hammett
Formation

Sycamore
Formation

Smithwick
Formation

Westcave area landscape 100,000 years ago. Birth of the ancestral Heinz Branch.
Illustration by S. Christopher Caran and Tim Hayes

channel, allowing the tributary channel of Heinz Branch to deepen rapidly.
The underlying Hammett Formation was soon fully exposed. Because the
Hammett is a soft shale, it eroded much faster than did the Cow Creek limestone. In fact, both the river and the branch quickly eroded the exposures
of Hammett shale along their banks, undercutting the layers of Cow Creek
rock and producing overhangs. This process may have created a high waterfall near the river, where ancestral Heinz Branch would have plunged over
the overhanging lip of Cow Creek limestone, wearing away the Hammett
shale even faster.

A waterfall is a knickpoint, or particularly steep segment of a stream
channel, and cannot remain stable indefinitely. The bed of hard Cow Creek
limestone at the top of the ancient falls would have created a knickpoint

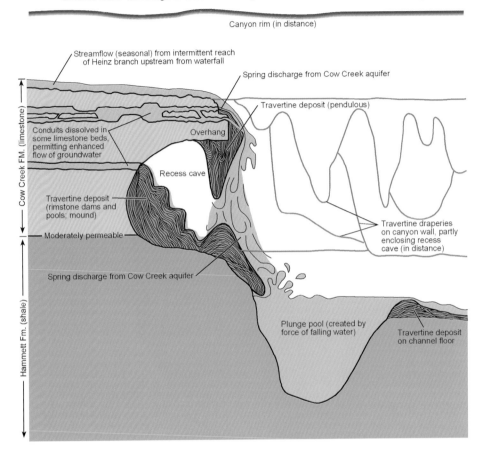

Ground-water discharge and travertine deposition at head of Heinz Branch canyon

Canyon rim (in distance)

Streamflow (seasonal) from intermittent reach
of Heinz branch upstream from waterfall

Spring discharge from Cow Creek aquifer

Travertine deposit (pendulous)

Cow Creek FM. (limestone)

Conduits dissolved in
some limestone beds,
permitting enhanced
flow of groundwater

Overhang

Recess cave

Travertine deposit
(rimstone dams and
pools; mound)

Moderately permeable

Travertine draperies
on canyon wall, partly
enclosing recess
cave (in distance)

Spring discharge from Cow Creek aquifer

Hammett Fm. (shale)

Plunge pool (created by
force of falling water)

Travertine deposit
on channel floor

Stream and spring flow at the waterfall and development of the grotto landscape.
Illustration by S. Christopher Caran and Joel Lardon

by resisting downcutting by the stream. Stream flow and spring discharge combined to form the cascading waterfall. The falling water eroded the softer, underlying Hammett shale, creating a recess beneath the prominent beds of hard Cow Creek limestone. Springs discharged from the porous limestone, causing the waterfall to remain active even when the usually inactive stream channel above the waterfall was dry.

Seepage from the Hammett Formation also enhanced erosion by weakening the exposed surface of these shale deposits, causing them to break into fragments. As the shale eroded, the Cow Creek layer was gradually undermined until the thick beds of limestone could not support their own

weight and fell off in huge blocks. A new waterfall developed a little farther upstream, but at the former waterfall's location the fallen blocks of
limestone covered the Hammett outcrop and partly protected it from further erosion. The canyon walls then eroded laterally, perpendicular to the
stream, but at a much slower rate because those slopes are mantled with
the limestone blocks, thus protecting the Hammett Formation downstream
from the knickpoint. The blocks also served to confine the stream midway
between the canyon walls, preventing the channel from meandering.

These factors created the straight, narrow, steep-walled canyon of ancestral Heinz Branch, much as it is today. Only at the head of the canyon,
beneath the waterfall, was the Cow Creek Formation continually undercut by rapid erosion of the Hammett shale. After Heinz Branch cut below
the base of the Cow Creek limestone at the new knickpoint, groundwater

50,000 Years Ago

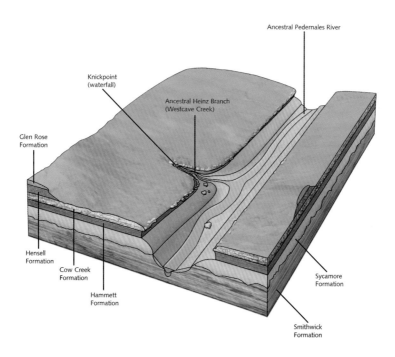

Westcave area landscape 50,000 years ago. The Pedernales River canyon is
entrenched, and Heinz Branch continues to evolve. Illustration by S. Christopher
Caran and Tim Hayes

Westcave Today

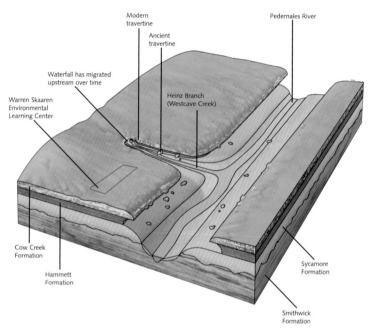

Westcave area landscape today. Illustration by S. Christopher Caran and Tim Hayes

drained out of that aquifer, further increasing stream flow. Thus, by perhaps fifty thousand years ago, ancestral Heinz Branch was flowing year-round.

This process has occurred many times over the past fifty thousand years, creating a succession of waterfalls moving up the canyon, with fallen blocks of limestone lining the lower part of the canyon. Today, the waterfall at the present head of the preserve's canyon is a spectacular sight. The falling water has eroded a deep pool surrounded by mounds and suspended masses of travertine beneath the waterfall.

Travertine Deposits

When groundwater moves through a limestone aquifer, it dissolves some of the surrounding bedrock. This process begins when rainwater and runoff seep into the aquifers through soils such as the thin Tarrant soil that develops on the Cow Creek Formation. Infiltrating water becomes mildly acidic and eventually reaches the Cow Creek aquifer.

Once within the Cow Creek limestone, the groundwater is enclosed in interconnected pores and small fractures. The groundwater is, therefore, under moderate pressure, which enhances its capacity to maintain its acidity. Both the Cow Creek limestone and the mineral binding the silt and sand grains within the underlying Hammett Formation are composed of calcite, a crystalline form of the chemical calcium carbonate. The acidic groundwater leaches away small amounts of calcite, gradually increasing the concentration of dissolved calcium carbonate in the groundwater.

Gradually, the concentration of dissolved minerals becomes very high. At the waterfall, physical and chemical changes occur when the groundwater emerges as a spring and is exposed to air, which reduces its ability to keep

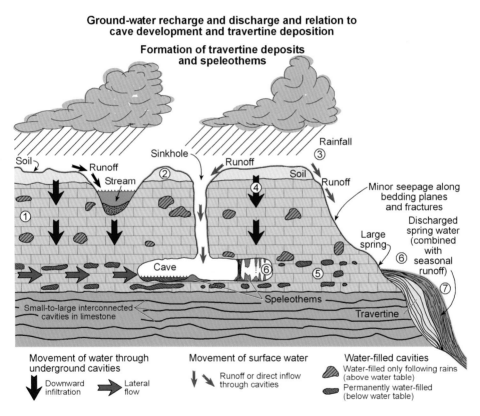

Ground-water recharge and discharge and relation to cave development and travertine deposition

Formation of travertine deposits and speleothems

Geological processes affecting aquifers and cave formation: bedrock (1) and soil (2) are infiltrated by precipitation, runoff, and streamflow (3), which flow vertically above the water table (4) and laterally below (5) creating caves and cavities; mineral-rich groundwater produces speleothems and travertine (6); spring flow (7) and runoff enhance stream flow. Illustration by S. Christopher Caran and Joel Lardon

A Note about Travertine

Visitors to Westcave Preserve take delight in the waterfall and the fanciful and extravagant mineral formations that decorate the grotto. These formations are composed of travertine, which forms the columns and undulating ribbons of stone that hang beneath the waterfall, coat the canyon walls, and create the enclosure that is the cave for which the preserve was named. When founding father John Covert Watson first saw the travertine wonders in the early 1960s, he thought of a "magic fairyland" or Valhalla.

The chemical reactions that produce these formations are complicated but fascinating. The process begins within the limestone beds that are exposed along the canyon rim at the top of the grotto waterfall. These beds are part of the Cow Creek aquifer, a body of rock containing groundwater. Wherever the aquifer is exposed, groundwater emerges, forming the perennial springs and seeps at the waterfall, within the cave and, to a lesser extent, at other points along the canyon walls downstream.

Acid Formation

Before discharging, however, the groundwater may remain within the aquifer for extended periods, sometimes many years, during which the water interacts with the rock medium chemically. In this region the ground seldom freezes to depths of more than an inch, and soils remain saturated only briefly after rains. Therefore, the near-surface horizons of most soils tend to be relatively dry and porous, allowing air to infiltrate. Soils contain organic carbon from materials such as particulate plant matter, pollen and fungal spores, liquid residues from plant decomposition, and insect and snail feces, known as frass and casts, respectively. The air within the soil oxidizes this material, forming carbon dioxide gas (CO_2) and water. The quantity of carbon dioxide in soil may be quite high, one hundred to one thousand times greater than in the atmosphere above ground. Carbon dioxide gas is denser than air and thus tends to move downward through the soil profile, filling tiny pore spaces and often dissolving in soil moisture. As rainwater, which is normally slightly acidic, permeates the soil, it dissolves some of the carbon dioxide gas and displaces the moisture already contained in pores. As it reacts with water, the CO_2 forms a dilute solution of carbonic acid (H_2CO_3).

Crystal Formation

The water recharging the Cow Creek aquifer is therefore mildly acidic. In a limestone aquifer, carbonic acid dissolves some of the bedrock with which it comes in contact. Limestone is principally composed of the mineral calcite, which is a crystalline form of the chemical calcium carbonate ($CaCO_3$). Reaction of the calcite mineral and carbonic acid increases the concentrations of ions of calcium (Ca^{2+}) and bicarbonate (HCO_3-) in the water, as shown by the chemical equation $CaCO_3 + H_2CO_3 \rightarrow Ca_{2+} + 2HCO_{3-}$.

As more groundwater moves into the aquifer after rain, the hydrostatic pressure increases slowly. The temperature of the groundwater is relatively constant and moderately low, approximately 68°F, which is close to the mean annual air temperature at the preserve, 67°F. Over the normal range of atmospheric temperatures at ground level, carbon dioxide gas is more soluble at low temperatures than at high. This property and the slightly elevated pressure of the groundwater allow the concentrations of ions to approach chemical saturation as long as the groundwater remains within the aquifer.

Chemical saturation means that for a given temperature and pressure, the concentration of ions has reached a maximum. Instead of dissolving additional calcium carbonate, the saturated water is then able to precipitate new mineral deposits. This happens spontaneously at the preserve when the groundwater discharges at springs and seeps. Upon emergence of the water, the sudden reduction in pressure and gradual warming (assuming the air temperature is greater than 68°F) tip the balance toward saturation, causing the formation of tiny crystals. Crystallization is further aided by a number of biological processes. Many cyanobacteria (also known as diatoms), algae, mosses, and other photosynthetic organisms are especially adapted to enhance the formation of calcite and another mineral, aragonite, which is also composed of calcium carbonate. The crystals coat the surfaces over which the water flows and, layer by layer, form the rock known as travertine.

Deposits at Westcave Preserve

Behind the waterfall a large travertine mound has accumulated over many years—perhaps hundreds—where the water flows and splashes. Upon inspection, the mound is seen to be covered with large tufts of moss and leaves fallen from trees above the canyon rim. If you touch the top of a moss tuft, it feels as you would expect: like a soft, wet plant. By touching the bottom, however, you will learn that the living moss is, in fact, being encased in travertine, literally fossilized before your eyes. Similarly, some of the leaves on the mound are flexible and may retain color, whereas others are rigid and covered in a thin layer of light gray crystals—and there are leaves in every stage in between. When the layer of crystals is thick enough, the leaf disappears entirely and is then permanently preserved within the mound. This process transpires in a matter of days. Although an impression of each leaf is retained inside the travertine deposit, there is soon little organic matter left. Fungi that specialize in consuming travertine-encased leaves and other biological materials are already at work and leave only a film of organic carbon. Travertine is not selective: fossilized insects, snails, diatoms (microscopic structures called frustules, which are composed of opal), even feathers have been found.

The cave contains other types of mineral accretions produced by groundwater seepage. Stalactites, stalagmites, rock draperies, and rimstone dams of varying size are present. The formation of these deposits, known as speleothems, is slower than accretion of the mound. Water flows over the mound continuously, whereas most of the speleothems were created one drip at a time. Yet the only real difference is that the volume of water required to deposit a single crystal moves more slowly in the cave.

those minerals in solution. As a result, new minerals crystallize, forming deposits known as travertine.

Mineral formations in caves, such as travertine, stalactites, and stalagmites, are called speleothems. Travertine deposits at springs are similar to other speleothems but generally form horizontal or sloping layers rather than vertical pendants or columns. Travertine also forms more quickly than stalactites and stalagmites at waterfalls and springs. Precipitation of calcite is so rapid that fallen leaves, aquatic plants living on the mound, and insects and other animal remains are trapped and preserved as fossils within the layers of travertine.

Travertine deposits drape the canyon walls along the overhang near the

Actively deposited travertine coats fallen leaves, seen in every stage of encrustation. Photo by S. Christopher Caran

preserve's waterfall and are so extensive that a section of the recessed overhang was walled off. This closed section forms the cave that gave Westcave Preserve its name. Seepage of springwater from the canyon rim caused the rapid accumulation of these travertine draperies. True stalactites and stalagmites, however, do form at the waterfall and within the cave wherever groundwater drips through pores and fractures in the ceiling of the overhang. This process could eventually fill the recess, but if the expanse of unsupported limestone is wide enough, the overhang could collapse before infilling is complete.

Landscape evolution continues even now. A few large fragments of travertine have broken away from the waterfall and canyon walls and can be seen surrounding the plunge pool, and there is a particularly large block of limestone near the waterfall.

In the canyon below the waterfall and pool the walls are partly coated with travertine deposits, the age of which appears to increase downstream. This indicates that the creation, partial infilling, and destruction of recesses

Travertine mound beneath waterfall with large stalactites and columns. Photo by S. Christopher Caran

such as the current cave have occurred many times as the canyon eroded steadily westward.

The existing waterfall has remained essentially stable since at least the late 1800s, but one day it, too, will collapse, and a new cycle of knickpoint development will begin still farther upstream. The complete cycle of evolution of the Westcave system is thus represented, providing evidence of geological and hydrological processes operating in concert over thousands of years. When you visit Westcave Preserve, you are seeing only one step in the long evolution of this dynamic landscape.

9 ❧ SURFACE WATER AND GROUNDWATER

> On the plateau summit their ultimate heads are gentle, waterless
> draws. . . . These lead down into deep . . . box canyons indenting
> the margin of the plateau . . . and at the bottom of which water
> begins to flow from gravity springs. The permanently flowing water
> of these canyons makes streams of great beauty.
>
> —Robert T. Hill, *Geography and Geology of the Black and Grand Prairies*
> *with Detailed Descriptions of the Cretaceous Formations and Special*
> *Reference to Artesian Waters* (1901)

The distinction between groundwater—water within the ground—and
surface water is somewhat artificial. Nearly all groundwater was originally surface water—rain, snowmelt, runoff, stream flow—that migrated
to an underground aquifer. Conversely, when groundwater discharges
from springs or seeps, it becomes surface water. There also is a transi-
tional stage. As stream water flows through its channel, it also permeates
the banks and the sediment on the channel floor. This infiltrating water
then flows underground at shallow depth and may emerge into the channel downstream. Known as hyporheic flow or interflow, this process is an
obvious example of the close relationship between groundwater and surface
water.

Surface Water

Waters at Westcave Preserve illustrate this interdependence. The surface
waters include:

- stream flow in upper Heinz Branch resulting from rainfall and runoff in the upper watershed;
- water in the plunge pool and stream flow in lower Heinz Branch

produced by spring discharge as well as flow from upper Heinz Branch;
- flow through the Pedernales River, from rainfall and runoff in the river's watershed;
- water from Lake Travis, when the lake level is sufficiently elevated because of rainfall and runoff in the Colorado River's watershed.

These waters affect the preserve in different ways. All have the potential to cause flooding.

The Heinz Branch watershed is just 6.2 miles long, covering 1,681 acres (2.6 square miles) in Blanco, Hays, and Travis Counties. Heavy rainfall over this area can cause flooding of upper Heinz Branch upstream from the waterfall. When that happens, the stream rushes toward the waterfall, combining with groundwater from the spring to produce a spectacular but violent cascade. That was the case on November 15, 2001, when the stream extended from bank to bank across the waterfall, and in October 2014 at about the same time as Austin's notorious Halloween Floods.

The force and turbulence of the flow scoured the plunge pool and eroded the sediment-filled channel downstream. Many of the smaller plants were stripped away, but they had largely recovered by the following spring. The resilience of the plants may be explained by the abundance and diversity of plant life and the normally genial environment, including constant spring flow and abundant soil moisture.

Springs

At the waterfall and along the canyon walls, numerous springs drain into the plunge pool, down the walls, or directly into the stream, increasing flow in the lower canyon. The springs may be the only source of water during particularly dry periods. The rate of flow at the main spring was measured on two such occasions. In 1955, during a severe drought, discharge was 0.19 liter per second, equivalent to 4,337 gallons per day. A second measurement was made in 1972, near the end of another extended but less extreme drought, when the flow was 0.63 liter per second, or 14,379 gallons per day. Although the discharge rates were unusually low at both times due to drought, this and perhaps other springs and seeps maintained at least minimal stream flow. Some sections of the stream may have appeared to be dry, but hyporheic flow continued.

As a result, the large trees and other plants in the canyon survived, almost entirely because of the emergent groundwater. A single mature Bald Cypress may use 880 gallons of water per day in summer, when it carries a full leaf canopy. Large Eastern Cottonwood and Pecan trees consume 500 and 350 gallons per day each, respectively. It is clear that an exceptionally prolonged episode of reduced spring flow could jeopardize even the canyon flora.

The Pedernales Effect

The Pedernales River is a major central Texas stream and one of the largest tributaries of the Colorado River. With a watershed area of 1,281 square miles, the river captures a significant volume of rainfall and runoff and has generated severe floods. The flood of record occurred in September 1952, ironically during the worst drought in central Texas history, which lasted from 1950 to 1956.

There are no gauged flood records from this part of the Pedernales Valley, but based on historic accounts and photographs, the estimated maximum river level at Hammetts Crossing during the 1952 flood was 50–70 feet above the bridge near Westcave Preserve. At a site approximately three miles downstream, a flood in 1869 caused a rise of 40–50 feet above the normal

Stream flow over the Westcave waterfall resulting from a rainstorm in October 2014 at about the same time as Austin's notorious Halloween Floods. Photo by Paul Vickery

river height. A rise of 50 feet at Hammetts Crossing would inundate the canyon floor of Heinz Branch almost to the plunge pool beneath the waterfall, and a flood level of 70 feet would have inundated the cave.

Conversely, the lower valley of the Pedernales River can at times be flooded by water flowing upstream from Lake Travis, where lake levels may fluctuate irrespective of rainfall and river conditions in the Pedernales watershed. When flowing, the Pedernales normally takes surface water to Lake Travis. Even if the Pedernales is flowing, the rising lake water may overwhelm the downstream flow and move upstream into the lower Pedernales Valley, causing what is called slack-water flooding. The most extreme examples of this type of flooding occurred in 1957, 1991, 1997, and 2007, as detailed in chapter 10, "Climate and Weather."

Over thousands of years the Pedernales River has carved a deep, relatively narrow, steep-walled canyon just east of Westcave Preserve. The canyon confines the rising waters, thus intensifying both river and lake flooding in this part of the river.

Fast-moving, turbulent floodwaters are able to transport large volumes of sediment. Most of the sediment in the lower part of the Pedernales drainage basin is derived from outcrops of hard limestone and chert, also known as flint. Indeed, the name Pedernales is the Spanish word for flint rocks. The river channel is filled with this highly durable, coarse gravel, which is porous and may be as much as thirty feet thick. Although the river bed sometimes appears to be dry, there is significant flow beneath the surface. The gravel-filled channel acts like a French drain, enabling the shallow groundwater to flow downstream through the porous gravel.

Groundwater

In the upper part of the watershed of Heinz Branch, groundwater behaves in a different manner. Rain falling on the hillsides seeps into the ground and moves vertically and laterally at a rate determined by the rock's permeability, which in turn is determined by the number and sizes of the open spaces and fractures and the connections among those openings. The limestone and lime-rich mudstone of the Glen Rose Formation absorb water slowly, but the clayey sandstone of the Hensell Formation allows rainwater and runoff to soak in quickly. The water not immediately absorbed becomes runoff, which eventually reaches the streambed of upper Heinz Branch, where it has additional opportunities for infiltration.

Looking into an aquifer: fractured Cow Creek limestone is exposed along the canyon rim. Infiltration of rainwater has widened the fracture. Photo by S. Christopher Caran

Aquifer Recharge

In a process known as aquifer recharge, water seeps downward through openings in rock, soil, and streambeds until it is cut off by less permeable layers. It then moves laterally but may encounter other open spaces extending downward. In the upper part of the Heinz Branch watershed, where the

Hensell sandstone is thickest, water infiltrating through the Hensell strata recharges the underlying Cow Creek aquifer. The thick, loamy Volente soil developed on the weathered Hensell helps to retain moisture and is an important source of water for vegetation during dry seasons.

In addition to receiving recharge through the Hensell Formation, the highly permeable Cow Creek limestone is also recharged directly, wherever it is exposed. Within this aquifer the water continues primarily downward until impeded by beds of shale in the Hammett Formation. This shale has a low absorption rate, which restricts further water penetration. Consequently, the lower part of the Cow Creek aquifer becomes saturated with groundwater. In places the saturated area may be more than twenty feet thick, but where the limestone beds are exposed along the rim of Heinz Branch canyon, the water drains out quickly, and the zone of saturation may be only a few feet thick.

This emergence of groundwater creates the perennial springs and seeps at the waterfall and cave and at other points along the canyon walls downstream. The continuous flow of water over the falls in dry weather is due solely to the springs. Thus, rainwater and runoff disappear into a recharge zone and flow as groundwater only to become surface water again when emerging at a spring. This water maintains the flow through lower Heinz Branch, below the waterfall, year-round.

10 ❧ CLIMATE AND WEATHER

Tongue cannot tell, nor can pen express, how cold a norther feels. . . .

—*Alexander Edwin Sweet, Texas writer and humorist (1841–1901)*

The words climate and weather are often regarded as interchangeable. In fact, these terms have different meanings, and the distinction between them is significant. Climate is the prevailing or long-term pattern of atmospheric conditions within a region or at a specific location, whereas weather is the state of the atmosphere in an area at a given time or over a short period. If we envision climate as a fabric, weather is an individual thread.

Air masses are extremely dynamic, and their properties and processes are impelled by a great many influences. Many of the same variables affect both climate and weather, particularly latitude, season, elevation and landform, proximity to the ocean or other water body, and ground cover. Increasingly, urbanization and human activities are also important and have both instantaneous and cumulative effects. This combination of global, provincial, and local factors governs the range of temperature, rainfall, humidity, cloudiness, wind speed and direction, and other atmospheric measures we experience annually and over many years, as well as the variations observed day-to-day and even minute-to-minute.

Overall, the climate of the preserve and most of central Texas is humid subtropical, with hot summers and relatively mild winters. Urbanization and other human activities in large cities produce microclimates that are usually warmer and more moist than conditions in the surrounding countryside. Westcave Preserve is sufficiently isolated that it is largely free from urban climatic influence. Of necessity, most of the records cited here are from weather stations located twenty to thirty miles to the east in Austin. There is, however, variation even across Austin, and the range of those conditions is reported when available.

Westcave Preserve

Location: Western Travis County, Texas

Latitude, longitude: Approximately N 30°20′30″, W 98°08′30″

Elevation: Approximately 690 to 850 feet above mean sea level

Climate: Subtropical humid to subhumid, hot summers, mild winters

Mean annual temperature (1951–80, estimated): 67°F

Mean annual daily maximum temperature (1951–80, estimated): 78°F

Mean annual daily minimum temperature (1951–80, estimated): 53°F

Mean annual precipitation (1951–80, estimated): 31.5 inches

Mean annual gross lake evaporation (1950–79, estimated): 64 inches

The following records are from the two nearest first-order weather stations, located in Austin, Texas, approximately 20 to 30 miles east of Westcave Preserve. The Mabry station is nearer and closer in elevation but is more affected by urban climatic conditions. Conditions at Westcave Preserve are approximated by the estimates above but are based in part on the data from Austin's weather stations.

	Austin Mabry	Austin Bergstrom
Average first freeze (1950–2012)	December 2	November 27
Earliest first freeze	October 26, 1924	October 25, 2005
Average last freeze (1950–2012)	February 23	March 4
Latest last freeze	April 9, 1914	April 17, 1999
Mean annual temperature (1981–2010)	69.3°F	67.2°F
Mean annual daily maximum temperature (1981–2010)	79.7°F	79.7°F
Mean annual daily minimum temperature (1981–2010)	58.9°F	54.8°F
Mean annual precipitation (1981–2010)	34.3 inches	32.2 inches
Maximum annual precipitation (year)	64.7 inches (1919)	55.7 inches (1957)
Minimum annual precipitation (year)	11.4 inches (1954)	10.0 inches (1954)
Mean monthly precipitation (1981–2010, range)	1.9 inches (July)–4.4 inches (May)	1.6 inches (August)–4.4 inches (June)

Latitude and Elevation

In the Northern Hemisphere, the Temperate Zone is that part of the planet between approximately 23.5° (Havana, Cuba) and 66.5° (southern edge of the Arctic Circle) north latitude. The latitude of Westcave Preserve is approximately 30° north, which is near the southern edge of the Temperate Zone. Therefore, the climate should be more like that of the Tropics than the Arctic. This part of Earth's surface is no different from other regions in that, in general, the seasonal changes in the number of hours of sunlight each calendar day have the greatest bearing on climate and weather, and the number of hours of sunlight is related to latitude. Latitude is, however, only one of the variables. The seasons, elevation, and landforms have significant effects as well.

At Westcave Preserve the elevation and landforms are similar to those of much of the Hill Country/Balcones Canyonlands area. Elevations within the preserve range from approximately 690 to 850 feet above mean sea level. The Westcave landscape includes a flat upland terrain, the narrow, steep-walled Heinz Branch canyon, and the broad valley of the Pedernales River.

Temperature

Temperature and rainfall have the most profound effects on the local environment. Summers are often hot, with an average daily high of 94.5°F, whereas the mean minimum temperature in winter is 37.6°F. There are, on average, 13.5 days with high temperatures of 100°F or greater per year and 19 to 25 days with temperatures of freezing or below. Because the uplands and wide Pedernales Valley are unprotected, these extremes can have an adverse effect on plants and animals, requiring special adaptations.

In contrast, conditions at the head of Heinz Branch canyon and downstream are moderated by shade in summer and sunshine in winter, as the deciduous trees gain or lose their leaf canopies. The steep canyon walls also create shade and a partly enclosed air space where moisture from spring flow and evaporation buffers the temperature variations. Air temperature in summer may be 10°F cooler in the canyon than in the adjacent Uplands. Cold air is sometimes trapped in the canyon in winter, resulting in below-freezing temperatures that persist for days, but such events are unusual.

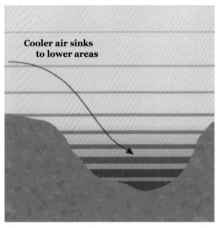

Air temperature in summer may be 10°F cooler in the canyon than in the adjacent Uplands. Illustration by Drew Patterson and Linda Wofford

Wind and Sun

In general, the Uplands and the Pedernales Valley are more exposed to wind and sun than is the protected Heinz Branch canyon, which is narrow and deep and oriented roughly east-west. Wind direction and velocity also vary seasonally. In winter, and to a somewhat lesser extent in autumn, the local climate is affected by conditions in the United States' continental interior. Winter winds are primarily from the north (as in the "norther" from the quotation at the beginning of this chapter) at an average maximum velocity of fifteen miles per hour, but winds also can come from the south. At other times of the year the wind is predominantly from the Gulf of Mexico, 170 miles to the southeast, with mean maximum velocities of fifteen to twenty-

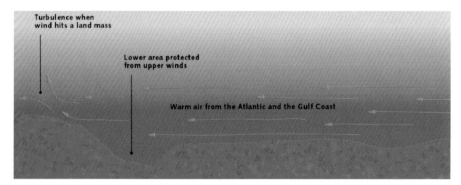

Westcave's canyon, which runs roughly east-west, is more protected from the predominant southeasterly winds than are the Uplands, which are exposed to turbulence and drying winds. In winter, the canyon also is protected from seasonal northerly winds. Illustration by Drew Patterson and Linda Wofford

five miles per hour. Therefore, winds generally blow over the Heinz Branch canyon rather than through it, although turbulence may cause windy conditions even there.

Rainfall

Rainfall is not notably subject to local conditions but may reflect regional influences. The mean annual precipitation varies from 32.2 to 34.3 inches across Austin, and monthly totals are distributed nearly evenly through the year. Mean monthly precipitation ranges from less than 2 to 4.4 inches, but the extremes are far more dramatic. Droughts may reduce the annual sum to as little as a third of normal, whereas in wet years the total may be nearly twice the average rainfall.

Floods

Flooding is more common in central Texas than in any other part of the continental United States. The rains that produce these floods usually are caused by tropical systems, especially in summer and autumn, and by cold fronts in spring. The highest monthly rainfall total in Austin was 20.8 inches in September 1921, and the resulting flooding was devastating.

This photograph was taken by S. D. Breeding in October after the September 11, 1952, flood of record when water rose an estimated fifty to seventy feet above Hammetts Crossing bridge near Westcave Preserve, scouring the Pedernales River canyon and destroying trees, including many Bald Cypress (*Taxodium distichum*). Photo courtesy of US Geological Survey

Flood control, plus the need for irrigation, hydroelectric power, and reliable sources of drinking water, led the Lower Colorado River Authority to construct six dams along the Colorado River northwest of Austin between 1935 and 1951, creating a chain of reservoirs known as the Highland Lakes. The Pedernales River empties into one of those reservoirs, Lake Travis.

Not all of these reservoirs provide flood control, but Lakes Buchanan and Travis are able to detain large volumes of floodwaters. The resulting new flood control system was severely tested September 9–11, 1952, when what was described as the "perfect storm and flood" caused water to race down the Pedernales and empty into Lake Travis. Lake level rose more than fifty feet in a twenty-four-hour period, and the Pedernales River was estimated to have risen fifty to seventy feet above the Hammetts Crossing bridge, causing epic destruction. Another memorable flood in the area in 2001 caused Heinz Branch to scour the plunge pool beneath the waterfall and strip vegetation and small trees growing in the lower canyon.

Flooding also may occur because of a rise in Lake Travis. In 1957, 1991, 1997, and 2007 Lake Travis sent water back up the Pedernales as far as the low-water bridge at Hammetts Crossing. On such occasions the bridge may remain underwater for months, and the mouth of Heinz Branch, just a stone's throw away, also is affected. During the Christmas Flood of 1991, for example, the river rose more than eighteen feet above the bridge for several months, and water backed up into Heinz Branch.

These kinds of events can alter wetland habitats. Many of the Bald Cypress, Pecan, and other large trees growing on the banks of the Pedernales near the low-water bridge were destroyed by the flood of 1952, and the woodland along the river has not yet fully recovered.

PART 3
The People

Horsetail (*Equisetum laevigatum*)
growing along stream. Illustration
by Nancy McGowan

11 ❧ ARCHEOLOGY AND HUMAN HISTORY

One cannot but imagine how these picturesque springs looked when they were being used as a home by early Americans.

—*Gunnar Brune, Springs of Texas (1981, 2002)*

Human chronology, particularly in the "new world" of the Americas, is divided into two eras, generally known as prehistorical and historical. This division is convenient and based on the nature of the records of the times. The events of prehistory are usually inferred through archeological investigations, whereas historical events are known from written accounts or other records. However, archeological methods are increasingly employed at historic sites.

The cave that gives Westcave Preserve its name was recorded as an archeological site in the 1930s, although few artifacts were recovered. The earliest occupation appears to have occurred during the Archaic Period (6000 BC to AD 800). Only limited archeological investigations have been conducted at the cave and at other similarly aged sites in and near Westcave Preserve. In 1959, excavations conducted within Heinz Branch canyon in and near the cave indicated the occasional presence of early humans. Occasional floods may have eroded artifact-bearing deposits, so it is possible that the record of prehistoric occupation is incomplete, but there is no physical evidence that the cave or canyon were used extensively by people before the modern era.

There is more evidence of prehistoric use on the drier Uplands, where erosion is less of a factor. In 1984 John Ahrns discovered a site on the northern rim of the canyon. This site and others were later surveyed by professional archeologists, who found evidence of flint tool manufacture but no datable artifacts. Archeologists with the Lower Colorado River Authority,

Noteworthy late Paleoindian projectile point circa 10,000 years before present found in the Westcave area. One third to one half of the artifact, including the tip, is missing. Note the fine parallel-flaked workmanship. Photo by Erich Rose

which owns Westcave, conducted additional surveys in 2012 and 2013, both of which found or documented previously known campsites, although none of these sites was determined to be significant.

Just south of the preserve an Early Archaic burned-rock midden was located and briefly investigated in 1977. Burned-rock middens are rock mounds where plant roots and other food items were baked. This site yielded Bulverde dart points, which date from 3000 to 1500 BC. Also found were some partially worked pieces, flint cores, and waste products from point and other tool manufacture.

A long history of uncontrolled relic hunting prior to establishment of the preserve may have damaged some sites, but there are no known sites of importance in the area. Today, the preserve prohibits excavation or disturbance of any object of antiquity.

Prehistoric Era

Considering the area's high value as a place to live, lying as it does in an area of remarkable biodiversity, it is little wonder that the history of human occupation here spans many thousands of years. Archeological investigations have provided a general understanding of the lifestyles of these prehistoric inhabitants of central Texas. Most of the evidence is based on interpretation of artifacts. Over thousands of years, toolmaking, acquiring and processing plant and animal resources, and other endeavors produced tangible byproducts—artifacts and other remains—that have survived to the present.

The time of the earliest habitation of this region is the subject of ongoing investigations, but we can state with some assurance that there are records of human presence in central Texas from at least fourteen thousand years ago. In this region the prehistoric era began with the first appearance of humans and continued until Europeans first explored Texas, about AD 1500. The earliest humans in central Texas probably formed small nomadic bands operating over very large territories. These groups may have hunted large herd animals almost exclusively, but the growing population became increasingly reliant on a variety of animal resources, including deer, land tortoises, aquatic turtles, alligators, and raccoons. Spring-fed streams in the Hill Country/Balcones Canyonlands region provided rich habitats and ready sources of water.

The prehistoric cultural era can be divided into four broad periods: Pre-Clovis, Paleoindian, Archaic, and Late Prehistoric. Because there is scant record of Pre-Clovis or Paleoindian habitation of the immediate area, the discussion of human prehistory here begins with the Archaic Period.

Archaic Period

The Archaic Period, from about 6000 BC to AD 800, is usually separated into three stages, Early (6000–2500 BC), Middle (2500–400 BC) and Late (400 BC to AD 800). A shift in technology is evident during the transition to the Archaic, with a change from lance-shaped projectile points to stemmed dart points. Artifacts recovered from Archaic sites include a variety of dart points used for hunting and tools such as manos and metates used to grind food items.

The atlatl appeared during the Archaic period. This device, a weighted shaft, was used to throw the short spears or darts for which the dart points were made. Dart points found at sites in the area of Westcave Preserve include Bulverde (Early Archaic), Travis (Middle Archaic), and Palmillas (Middle to Late Archaic). There is evidence of intensive plant processing during the Early Archaic, as well as continued reliance on a relatively small number of animal species, including deer, turkey, and amphibious and aquatic vertebrates.

By the Middle Archaic, populations were increasing and needed more plant resources, particularly acorns, cactus tunas, wild onions, pecans, walnuts, Agarita berries, grapes, plums, and persimmons. Remains of the modern species of bison are poorly represented at Early Archaic sites in this region but are more common at Middle Archaic sites. There was an apparent increase in artifact diversity during the Middle Archaic, with the addition of woodworking and boneworking implements and tools that appear to have supported bison hunting. Burned-rock middens became an even more prominent feature at archeological sites throughout the region.

The Late Archaic population appears to have risen even higher, and there is a suggestion of established tribal territories based on the adoption of simple burial practices and establishment of cemeteries. Bison remains continued to be common, especially at sites in the prairies east of the Edwards Plateau but also in parts of the Hill Country near Westcave Preserve that had ready sources of water. Here were areas of grassland interspersed with stands of oak and other trees. The human inhabitants continued to consume a wide variety of plants, but as before, they used only a limited number of animal species. Known archeological sites include open campsites and procurement areas for chert and other rock types used to make stone tools.

Late Prehistoric Period

This period ranges from AD 800 to about 1500. The Late Prehistoric was characterized by a continuation of the hunter-gatherer lifestyle and use of burned-rock middens. There were, however, a number of significant changes in material culture. The most notable was in weapon technology through replacement of the dart and atlatl and introduction of the bow and arrow.

Other developments occurred late in this period, including the first use of ceramics and limited agriculture in some areas. The latter is poorly documented in central Texas and may have been highly localized. A type of pottery known as plainware that is often associated with agricultural societies has been found at sites in the region. The wide range of natural resources available to the region's inhabitants may have made agriculture less necessary here than elsewhere.

The wooded hills and valleys of the Edwards Plateau to the west and prairies to the east offered diverse resources exploited during seasonal rounds of hunting and gathering. Favorable environmental factors included a moderate climate, numerous springs and streams, and plentiful game and plants. This was the nature of central Texas encountered by the first Europeans to enter the region. For the indigenous inhabitants, however, the arrival of the Europeans meant that a lifestyle that had existed for thousands of years would soon change forever.

Historic Era

In central Texas, specifically in proximity to Westcave Preserve, the effects of European exploration and immigration were delayed somewhat longer than in the southern, eastern, and far western parts of the state. For this reason, the time from about AD 1500 to 1750 may be called the Protohistoric Period, because direct European influence was limited and its impact was transitory.

Europeans were present in ever-increasing numbers throughout this interval, and by the 1700s multiple generations of their descendants had been born in the Americas. In Texas, permanent settlements were established at El Paso and a number of locations in southern and eastern Texas. Yet there were few and only brief incursions into central Texas north of San Antonio, which was then the northern fringe of the province of New Spain. Colonial residents had little interaction with the indigenous peoples of the region, although that would change. By the beginning of the Historic Period, about 1750, the Spanish and others were present in such overwhelming numbers that the transition to European-derived ways of life was all but complete.

Protohistoric Period

Events occurring well outside of central Texas had extensive and enduring effects on the inhabitants of this region, through the activities of the Spanish to the west and south and, to a lesser extent, the French to the east. These two great powers clashed on battlefields in Europe and on the seas and over their colonial ambitions in the Americas. The Spanish were particularly successful, because they were funded with the riches of the Aztecs of Mexico and Incas of Peru and from new silver mines operating in both areas.

After the Spanish settled in what is now New Mexico and northern Mexico, they began to explore Texas and came into contact with local Native American hunter-gatherer populations and the settled agricultural communities of the Caddoan peoples of eastern Texas and areas to the north. The written accounts of these explorers provide the first descriptions of the environment and its inhabitants, including the names of various native groups. Evidence of this early contact includes European-made metals, glass, and other materials recovered from archeological sites of the period. An indirect effect of the European presence was the spread of diseases that had not previously existed in the Native American populations, such that even at this early date the population of indigenous peoples was in decline.

The Native American groups in and around central Texas were changing in other ways as well. Whole populations were on the move. Some were escaping northward from forced labor at the mines and ranches of northern Mexico. Others, particularly the Wichitas, were moving south and west from eastern Texas and Arkansas to avoid conflicts with other Native American groups.

One of the most significant causes of change was the introduction of horses, which were previously unknown in the New World. As Native Americans quickly became skilled riders, their entire culture evolved almost overnight. The Lipan Apaches and Comanches were particularly affected and spread eastward and southward from their former homelands in the foothills of the Rocky Mountains to the northwest. They began hunting bison on horseback and were soon raiding other Native Americans across the Great Plains to the east and Spanish settlements as far south as San Antonio. With their horses, and guns supplied by the French beginning in the late 1600s, the Lipan Apaches displaced many other groups, who in turn relocated, altering the lifestyles of the inhabitants of other areas. This ripple effect modified the cultural landscape of the region.

By the middle 1700s the relocation and merging of Native American cultures had reached central Texas. The Apaches were the first of these new groups in the area but were expelled by the Comanches, who would later be driven from the region by the westward expansion of Anglo-Americans. Given the location of Westcave Preserve along the Pedernales River, a normally reliable water source, there is at least the potential for discovery of archeological sites preserving artifacts from the period of contact, when Native Americans first encountered European explorers. Groups with formerly separate cultural identities replaced one another in waves or melded into new forms, and all were adapting to a new, European-influenced lifestyle.

Historic Period

With San Antonio well established by the middle 1700s, the Spanish were able to explore what had been terra incognita just to the north. Central Texas was rumored to contain silver, gold, and other minerals, and several attempts were made to discover these riches. One such expedition was undertaken by Bernardo de Miranda, who left San Antonio in early 1756 and proceeded northward to a reported site of silver ore. The route crossed the Pedernales River approximately sixteen miles west of Westcave Preserve. The expedition finally reached its destination in what is now Llano County and collected samples that were submitted for assay.

Miranda's report of his finds was wildly exaggerated, stating that the amount of silver ore was so great that a mine could be given to every inhabitant of the province of Texas. In fact, no silver was recovered. Nonetheless, there followed numerous attempts to locate the mine and other sites of mineral wealth. Even historical figures of no less weight than Stephen F. Austin and Jim Bowie were among the willing participants in this search.

The exact location of Miranda's prospecting site has been disputed, but it was probably southeast of the present-day city of Llano in Llano County. Many of the later explorers undoubtedly followed the route of the Miranda expedition, fording the Pedernales at the same location. The lure of great riches remained the primary reason for traveling through this part of the state until the mid-1800s.

Spanish colonial control of the region continued through the eighteenth century, but with little additional impact on central Texas. The first decades of the 1800s were particularly eventful in the history of the region. Mexico, which then included Texas, won its independence from Spain. Spanish descendants known as Tejanos established a thriving economy largely founded on cattle ranching. Anglo-American and later German settlers streamed into the region in increasing numbers, and in less than fifty years Texas became an independent republic and later a state in the United States.

There is little information about the history of the Westcave area itself until the 1840s, when homesteading began in the area.

12 ❧ WESTCAVE, 1850–1974

In the mid-1800s "the middle of nowhere" adequately described the area near what is now Westcave Preserve. Steep cliffs along the Pedernales River meant no crossing there. The stagecoach from Austin to Fredericksburg (a four-day trip of ninety miles on rocky, rutted dirt roads) forded the river about eight miles upstream, at Dead Man's Crossing. There was no "closest town," and the nearest fort was Fort Martin Scott near Fredericksburg, fifty miles away and little more than a forage depot. This was the Wild West— the skirmish line of civilization—with wildfires, drought, Indian attacks, wolves, coyotes, mountain lions, bears, and rattlesnakes to contend with.

In 1849, Mormon homesteaders arrived at Cypress Mill Springs, eight miles northwest, establishing, then soon abandoning a sawmill for cypress lumber and relocating. It was not until 1857 that German settlers established Fuchs Mill (later renamed Cypress Mill), a gristmill on Cypress Creek just downstream from the original Mormon site.

The Hammetts and Hamiltons

Among the earliest Anglo settlers in the area were the Hammett and Hamilton families. The 1860 census shows them owning property and making a living by farming or raising stock. Sheep were favored, as wool could earn high prices, and cotton was a major cash crop in the area from about 1870.

The Hamiltons lived east of the Pedernales River, across the river and northeast of what the locals called either West Cave or West Caves, as it was west of the river. They built a cabin on the south side of Hamilton Creek, a tributary of the Pedernales that has become famous for its dazzling fifty-foot waterfall and grotto named Hamilton Pool, which regularly makes the list of the country's best swimming holes.

The brothers Washington and Blue Hammett owned land on both sides of the Pedernales and built a stone house on the east side of the river. Washington had been a first lieutenant in the Rio Grande Squadron of the Texas Rangers, then a captain in the First Texas Cavalry during the Civil

The State of Texas,

COUNTY OF *Hays*   BEFORE THE UNDERSIGNED authority personally

appeared *J. B. Hammett* applicant, and *Wash Hammett* and *Jas G. Townsend*

who being duly sworn according to law, declare that *J B Hammett*

is **Bona Fide** settled upon vacant public domain, (the same described in the accompanying file) under *"An Act to regulate the Disposal of Public Lands of the State of Texas,"* approved the 12th day of August, 1870, and that he has not a Homestead. *& has been on & improving it since August 1. 1882*

J B Hammett

Wash Hammett

J G Townsend

Sworn to and subscribed before me, this *4th* day of *October* 1882

IN TESTIMONY WHEREOF, I hereunto affix my official Seal and signature.

Ed J L Green

Clk. Co. ct. Hays Co Texas

DESIGNATION.

To the *County* Surveyor of *Hays County* — :

By Virtue of the accompanying Affidavits, No ___ made in accordance with the first section of *"An Act to regulate the Disposal of the Public Lands of the State of Texas,"* approved the 12th day of August, 1870, I hereby apply for a Survey of the following premises, to wit:

Beginning at the S W Corner of the Wash Hammett preemption — Thence S.E. on his line to the Buas R.R. survey — Thence South the line of same to the Hancock land — Thence West down the Hancock line to the Perdinales river — Thence down said Perdinales river to the beginning — so as to contain 80 acres within said bounds —

J B Hammett

Land grant conveying ownership of eighty acres from the State of Texas to J. B. Hammett on October 4, 1882. Image from Texas General Land Office

117

War. Local family histories mention that at one time there was a cable across the river near West Cave to assist in crossing the river. By the early 1870s the Hammetts had blasted out part of the one-hundred-foot cliffs to make way for a descent by road to a rocky low-water crossing about fifty feet downriver from the present bridge. They charged a toll, which was worth paying, as the new Hammetts Crossing saved about half a day's journey from Austin to and from the thriving Cypress Mill (eight miles), Round Mountain (fifteen miles), and Llano further northwest. The new roadway also brought more business to Austin. By 1874 the US postal service and stagecoach used Hammetts Crossing on the route called the Austin-Llano road.

In Round Mountain in 1874 the widow Elitha Martin built a two-story stone hotel next to a livery stable to provide food and rest for stagecoach passengers. Still known as the Round Mountain Stagecoach Inn (on the National Register of Historic Places), it is near what is now US 281 and Texas Ranch Road 962. Soon after 1880, the stagecoach line on the Austin-Llano road ceased to operate on this route, probably because of competition from the Austin and Northwestern Railroad, which hauled passengers and mail as well as pink stone from Granite Mountain for construction of the new Capitol building in Austin.

At river level the

The cave at Westcave Preserve, first known as West Cave. The photo is by William J. Oliphant, a photographer in Austin from 1866 to 1880. PICA 25895, Austin History Center, Austin Public Library

new road at Hammetts Crossing ran by the mouth of the canyon that led to West Cave. Word spread that hiking a quarter mile to the head of the canyon would be rewarded with a view of a fern-draped emerald pool with a forty-foot waterfall and a cave draped in beautifully grotesque ribbons of rock. The graffiti "BL [or RL] Nichols, July 21, 1883, Bastrop TX," is cut into a stone just inside the cave entrance. The inscription is still visible and is pointed out during tours of the preserve. Also, a half dime, a five-cent silver coin that was discontinued in 1873, has been found near the cave, helping to date early visits.

The 1880s

By the 1880s Cypress Mill, just eight miles to the northwest, was the largest town in the area. Although Bee Caves, about fifteen miles east, was also close, it was relatively small. Both towns had a gristmill, a cotton gin, a post office (Bee Caves in 1873, Cypress Mill in 1874), and a school, but Bee Caves had 20 residents and Cypress Mill had 130.

Minna Goebel, a niece of the founder of the mill at Cypress Mill, remembered the dangers of life on the frontier:

Of course there were plenty of wolves and wildcats. Often during lambing time, the shepherd couldn't bring all the sheep in. I remember one time just about sundown we walked about one half mile or more up a hill, and down below us on the other side were sheep stomping their feet. Then we could see a wolf trying to catch a lamb; the old ewes wouldn't let him. I guess if we hadn't come he would have caught it. . . . The wolves and wildcats were so bad. We often caught wild cats in traps, by putting a chicken in a coop and setting the traps around them.

In the summer of 1880 Hermann Lungkwitz, a German-born photographer and landscape artist whose work became the first pictorial history of the Texas Hill Country, undertook a sketching tour of the Pedernales River valley, commissioned by the Texas General Land Office. He captured precious images of "West Cave," Hamilton Pool, and Hammetts Crossing using oil on canvas and pencil on paper.

Lungkwitz is thought to have stayed with the John L. Buaas family at their ranch near Hamilton Pool, which Buaas bought in 1879 from J. M. Hammett. A native of Norway, Buaas came to Austin before the Civil War

Painting by Hermann Lungkwitz of Westcave grotto, ca. 1880. Note the pair of human figures at center for scale. Estate of Walter and William Staehely; James Patrick McGuire, Hermann Lungkwitz: Romantic Landscapist on the Texas Frontier (1983)

and opened an entertainment center called Buaas's Hall on East Sixth Street. Lungkwitz gave one of his drawings the German name "Buaas Quellweg" (Buaas Crossing), but later it was renamed "Road to Capt. Hamit Crossing of the Pedernales."

By 1900, Henry Reimers and family had acquired the Hamilton land, pool, and adjacent property totaling about three thousand acres in the Pedernales River valley. Henry and Dora Reimers were German immigrants who had arrived in 1882 and first settled at Shovel Mountain, then in nearby Cypress Mill. Henry worked at the mill for five years and began buying land, much of it east of the Pedernales. The couple built a stone house near the present site of Hamilton Pool. They set up the one-room Hamilton Pool School in 1886 on their ranch and hired teachers, who boarded in their home.

The Reimers' descendants would eventually own about ten thousand acres in the area and operate Hamilton Pool as a commercial recreation

Hamilton Pool School, 1927. Kneese family photo

Some Hamilton Pool School students, from left: Bernice Hunnicutt, Florene Bond, Elnora Neumann, and J. D. Lawson. The teacher is Ruth Hunnicutt Haynes. Kneese family photo

area. In 1985, Travis County purchased 232 acres from the Reimers family and established Hamilton Pool Preserve as part of its parks system. In 2006 Travis County used bond money to establish the 2,427-acre Milton Reimers Ranch Park located near Hamilton Pool Preserve.

Lottie's Wedding

On Christmas Day 1904 a wedding took place at Hammetts Crossing. Charlotte Pauline (Lottie) Wilke, the daughter of Emil and Frances Wilke, who lived on the Hamilton Pool side of the river, married Wilhelm Heinrich Gustave Kroll. The oldest of eight children, Lottie was born September 23, 1887, in Travis County, and she lived to age ninety-four. Her granddaughter Shirley Weirich said that in later years Lottie liked to visit the spring near Hammetts Crossing where as a girl she had fetched water for the family.

Shirley's favorite story about her grandmother was that Lottie loved to read, "but her daddy would fuss at her about putting the oil lamp out and going to bed because she was using too much oil." So Lottie would wait until her family was asleep, hide in a closet, light the lamp, and continue to read her books. Shirley says her grandmother had only a third-grade education, but she read and traveled all her life and was knowledgeable about many things, probably thanks to her love of books.

Wilhelm Heinrich Gustave Kroll and Charlotte Pauline (Lottie) Wilke were married at Hammetts Crossing in 1904. Wilke family photo

The Adventuresome Coverts

In the 1910s and '20s the adventuresome Covert family, who were large landowners in the Austin-Bastrop corridor and had opened an Austin car dealership in 1909, began motoring out to Hamilton Pool. Others also enjoyed picnicking at the scenic outpost, but the Covert name is noteworthy, as it was John Covert Watson, born in 1929, who would be instrumental in establishing the nature preserve that exists today. Watson grew up going on family excursions near the Pedernales River, but it was not until the early 1960s that he first visited what would become Westcave Preserve.

A favorite story that Watson heard when he was a boy came straight from his Aunt Ninny (Katherine Covert Temple). She was fond of recounting her slip and fall into the Pedernales River, holding firm to her parasol and with all her petticoats on. She almost drowned because it took the men she was with so long to unbutton their boots and go in to rescue her.

Ward, Von Rosenberg, and Granville Ownership

By the early 1900s ownership of the land once held by the Hammetts on the west side of the river had passed to Antonette and J. D. Ward. On October 7, 1920, the Wards sold what is now Westcave Preserve to Carl J. Von Rosenberg. In the agreement is the stipulation that Ward "be permitted to use the cotton field until Dec. 15, 1920" and "reserves the right to cut and haul off all cypress and cedar timber in the bottom land" of a certain dimension for four years, "with the exception of an 8½ acre tract known as 'the Gulch.'" It seems likely that "the Gulch" refers to the canyon at the heart of the current Westcave Preserve.

Von Rosenberg was a merchant banker and state legislator from a prominent family who had emigrated from Prussia through Galveston and settled in Fayette County. After acquiring the property, he was an absentee landowner, leasing the land to others who raised livestock and grew cotton and corn, which the land would support. Von Rosenberg died in 1934 and passed the land on to his grandson C. J. Granville, who was a child prodigy pianist and continued as an absentee landlord until selling the land in 1937 to Chester F. Lay (see "The Lay Ranch").

Ladies and a gentleman at Hammetts Crossing in 1910 using the stones as a bridge. Source unknown

A Copperhead and a Grave

One of the families in the early 1900s who "lived on places and worked for people," according to their grandson Bobby Wilson, was a couple named Ella Crawford and Andrew (Jack) Madison. They worked the land above the grotto, now called the Uplands, and lived in the board-and-batten wood cabin that still exists. Wilson, who owns a ranch between Hammetts Crossing and Cypress Mill, remembers vividly his grandmother's story about the copperhead snake that bit her and caused her to miscarry. "She told me she buried the baby on the land, next to Blue Hammett," said Wilson in 2015 during an interview for this book.

A small unmarked cemetery associated with the cabin has been the subject of local legend for many years. It is said to have been fenced at one time and located under a cluster of oak trees northeast of the cabin. One story says that the gravesite contains the remains of a female Hammett and her baby. Another says an unidentified woman bitten by a copperhead snake is there. Yet another story says that Owen family members are buried there. The Owen connection was disclosed by a visitor to Westcave Preserve in the 1990s who claimed to be a distant relative of the person(s) buried there and showed preserve manager John Ahrns the reported burial location where several cedar posts lay on the ground under trees.

Later, Ahrns received a note identifying the graves as those of Luke Owen, March 8, 1849–March 12, 1910, and Mary Alice Owen, December 29, 1854–February 21, 1910. Archeological investigations in 2013 by the Lower Colorado River Authority (LCRA), which leases the land to Westcave, found that Luke Owen disappeared from census records after 1880, and his wife, Mary, was still living in 1920. The graves of both were conclusively located on nearby Reimers Ranch, east of the Pedernales River.

Because of the uncertainty regarding the Owen cemetery, the Texas Historical Commission recommended that the gravesite not be formally recorded. Bobby Wilson, the grandson of Ella Crawford, who told him she buried her baby on the land, has no doubt that there is a Crawford grave somewhere on the property. Wilson knows his grandmother would not have made a mistake about where she put her child in the ground. He was never taken to the gravesite, so the Crawford plot may or may not be in the same location as the Owen plot that was shown to Ahrns in the 1990s.

Duval Family and Panthers in the Cave

A childhood memory of those days comes from Claiborne A. Duval Jr., who remembers that in the 1920s "we frequently walked from the house bare-footed and in bathing suits (standard summer attire) down the path that entered the canyon from above between the large pool and upper spring pools. One of these small pools is where we put melons to make them cold. One of those small upper pools was deeper than we were tall." He remembered that one day his aunt ran ahead of the family into the mouth of the cave and "immediately came out followed by a panther."

Betty Duval Burton wrote in a letter dated 1997 that in "about 1931 or 1932" her Duval family rented a small farmhouse above the waterfall: "Our biggest treat was to walk from the farm across fields and meadows full of wildflow-ers, thistle and nettles. We'd come down from above like billy goats and enjoy the waterfall, the deep waterhole and the small pools on the ledge above for the smaller children. We never saw anyone else there. It was our own 'magic land.' My brothers and cousins told us of the panthers in the caves and how we would never be found if we drowned in that deep deep pool."

Building the Bridge

In 1925 the location of what had been the shallow, rocky Hammetts Crossing ford was moved about fifty feet upriver and improved to become a low-water bridge. Plans filed with Travis County dated July 1924 show "Bridge #315 Hammett's Crossing Low Water Concrete Steel Bridge" with two approaches. O. Leonard was the design engineer. The plans show piers sunk into rock, a plan view, and a profile, with the bridge twenty feet wide and eighty feet long—four spans of twenty feet each (19 feet 6 inches).

Oral histories from the Neumann and Burleson families indicate that local landowners and residents were asked for donations to construct the bridge and that they helped with the actual construction. Arthur Neumann told his daughters that he and other men grubbed out large cypress trees from the banks by hand and with the help of their mules. Then the mule skinners hauled sand and gravel from nearby, mixed it with cement and river water, and carried the concrete bucket by bucket to fill in forms. The bridge retains pieces of travertine and quartz from the gravel mix. Holton Burleson remembered that on the day of the official bridge opening, the whole community gathered on the bridge for a picnic.

The new bridge would be underwater many times when the river was high but would stand up through repeated flooding. The bridge meant an easier and safer road for ranchers driving cattle to the railhead and taking goods to market in Austin. Before the new bridge, it would take the Neumann family, who lived a few miles west of the crossing, two days to travel to Austin for supplies. They would spend the night in a wagon yard before returning home the next day. After completion of the new bridge, the family splurged on a Model T Ford. Families with children living west of the river would no longer have to put up with their children fording the river to get to and from the Hamilton Pool School on the east side.

Taking the "Near Cut" through West Cave

One such schoolgirl was Elnora Neumann, who was born in 1921. Her older sisters Olivia and Hilda used the ford before the bridge was built in

Hammetts Crossing bridge in 2015. Photo by Elaine Davenport

1925, walking a total of six miles and crossing the river twice each day to get to and from school. Hilda remembered having to take off her shoes and socks to wade the river or jump from stone to stone. By 1927, when Elnora reached school age, the bridge had been built and life was a little easier—a fact that Elnora's older sisters did not let her forget.

West Cave, as it was then known, was located between the Neumann home and school. "As we walked to school, we did not always follow the road," said Elnora Neumann Kneese in a video interview with Ric Sternberg and Sue Barnett in 2004:

We took as many near-cuts through as we could to make the distance shorter. We cut through many times on the bluff owned by the West Cave. There was two big rocks and a big crevice where a trail went in between. We went down through that trail. It was always spooky to me. I always thought a panther or lion would jump on me sometimes, as there was some in and around our country at that time. Sometimes on our way home from school we would go up into the West Cave and get a drink of water, as the spring water there was always nice and cool. But our parents had forbidden us to do this because there were steps that came on out to the top of the cave. These steps were small, slippery and dangerous. They were afraid we would slip and fall and hurt ourselves or fall into the big pool of water that was at the cave which during these days man could not find the bottom of the pool.

Flash Floods, the Neighborhood Character

According to the LCRA: "The Hill Country and Central Texas have a greater risk of flash flooding than most regions of the United States. The region is called Flash Flood Alley because of the area's steep terrain, shallow soil, and unusually high rainfall rates. Heavy rains can quickly transform into walls of fast-moving water with great destructive potential." For the area's residents, the floods were a quirky, dangerous, awe-inspiring neighborhood character who turned up from time to time with little warning and changed their lives. Elnora remembers:

We usually stopped at the Bonds, to and from school, as it was on our way. Their three girls—Florene was about my age—would walk with us to school. Many times we did not get to school when there was a big rain and the Pedernales River was up over the bridge. We came

Floodwaters cover the low-water bridge at Hammetts Crossing, spring 2015. Photo by Paul Vickery

Florene Bond, age fourteen (left), and Elnora Neumann, age thirteen, at Hammetts Crossing in 1934. Kneese family photo

back home. Sometimes, Mr. Lee Bond would go down to the river and take us across on his horse, if the water was not too swift for the horse to wade across. He would have to take one at a time. Usually, there was five or six of us kids. We only would do this if the water was falling, not rising, as if it was rising, it is very dangerous. We were always warned never to get close to the river when it was raining, because it would come down in a roll and it would just catch you.

From time to time the neighborhood had to contend with a raging roll of muddy water that came down the Pedernales River. A record high flood was reported in July 1869 near Johnson City, twenty miles upstream from Hammetts Crossing. Subsequent great floods took place in May 1929 and in June 1935. From September 9 to 11, 1952, in the middle of the 1950–56 drought, known as the worst drought in Texas history, the area was inundated with twenty-three inches of rain in twenty-four hours in what became the flood of record in this part of the Pedernales Valley. Upstream, the US 281 bridge over the Pedernales at Johnson City was destroyed, while at Hammetts Crossing a line of flood debris on the cliffs indicated that water had risen fifty to seventy feet above the bridge. The bridge survived the flood, but the riverbanks were stripped of many ancient Bald Cypress trees that had withstood previous major floods.

Elnora Neumann Kneese, who was married with a child of her own by then and living close to where she was born, remembers vividly the Great Flood of 1952. A beloved grove of Pecan trees half a mile upstream from the bridge "just washed away: I went down there and it was everything under water. And it took away all of our beautiful trees—cypress trees, and all of the pecan trees." She remembers the "beautiful sandbar" that had long been a favorite picnic destination: "A couple of neighbors and us would go down there some afternoons. And we'd fix our supper. We'd fry bacon and potatoes with a little sand—a little sand and a little ashes—oh, but it was good!"

The quirky neighborhood character turned up again during the Christmas Flood of 1991, when Hammetts Crossing bridge was more than eighteen feet under water. That flood closed the bridge for months and backed water up the Pedernales River from Lake Travis into the Heinz Branch canyon. Neighbors remember that John Ahrns became the local mailman, paddling across the placid lake formed by the flooded river to the mailboxes on the Austin side and returning with everyone's mail.

The Lay Ranch

Chester Frederick Lay, an accounting and management professor at the University of Texas at Austin, and his wife, Harriet, bought the land that would become the preserve on April 29, 1937. On a résumé, Lay listed "owner-manager of a small Texas ranch" among his nonacademic activities and his personal interests as ranching, travel, hunting, quarter horses, and family, state, and local history.

Lay's daughter-in-law Madeline remembers annual trips to what they called the Lay Ranch from their Florida home. They stayed in the ranch house—which had been used on and off since the early 1900s—on the uplands plateau above the grotto. There was no electricity, no running water, and an outhouse. They luxuriated in the travertine pools under the

Chester and Harriet Lay at the Lay Ranch, as they called the Westcave land during their ownership from 1937 to 1966. Lay family photo

waterfall, one of which they proudly dubbed the Queen's Bathtub. It was the biggest and the most prized of the pools. Of course, they heard tall tales of cowboy bank robbers who had taken refuge in the cave and the possibility of buried treasure there.

Madeline's son Coy Lay Jr. remembers visiting the "wonderland" as a boy and diving off a big rock into the pool. He also remembers cold, slippery expeditions inside the cave, heading for the window of light beneath the waterfall. Coy's older sister Gretchen Randolph has fond memories of an open-faced, two-story treehouse near the cabin.

Coy Lay Jr. and his grandfather Chester Lay at their treehouse on the Lay Ranch. Lay family photo

A fine quarter horse named Lady, which the grandchildren were told came from the King Ranch in South Texas, was kept at the property. Gretchen remembers riding Lady into the nearby field to pick ears of corn for the family's dinner. Coy admits to being bucked off—a fate that did not occur when Coy was much younger and rode one of the cabin's porch rails with a saddle strapped to it. That photo of the cloth-diapered baby buckaroo was a favorite of Coy's mother, Madeline.

One of Gretchen's favorite stories was of her mother fighting off a rattlesnake with a flyswatter: "We were taking a bath on the back porch. My grandfather had rigged a rain collection system, and we were in a big tin tub. A rattlesnake came out from underneath the house. I remember very clearly my mother going after that rattlesnake with a flyswatter. She got between us and the rattlesnake, who must have understood he was up against an angry mother. I'm just glad she wasn't hurt."

Born in Illinois in 1895, Chester Lay held degrees in education, economics, and business administration from Illinois State University in Bloomington and the University of Chicago. He spent nineteen years at the

Coy Lay Jr. riding the porch rail at the ranch house that Westcave now calls the Historic Homestead. Coy's mother Madeline favored this photo. Lay family photo

Madeline Lay and daughter Gretchen in happier times, when Madeline was not going after a rattlesnake with a flyswatter to protect her children. Lay family photo

University of Texas at Austin (UT) as a professor and also as head of personnel and management. Lay left UT in 1945 to become president of Southern Illinois University in Carbondale. He resigned in 1948 and went to Southern Methodist University in Dallas from 1948 to 1959 as chairman, professor, and director of Graduate Studies in Administration and Management of the School of Business. He finished his academic career at Trinity University in San Antonio. Lay wrote numerous articles for professional and educational journals and was a national officer in several educational and business societies. The Business Management Honor Society recognized Lay as one of the three leading professors of business administration who had contributed most to the teaching of business in American universities.

When the time came to sell the land, Gretchen remembers that her grandfather was concerned about the canyon. He knew it was "extremely unusual" and wanted it protected. He was frustrated because he could not persuade the Audubon Society to buy it. Lay sold the property in 1966 to W. D. Nicholson, a family physician from Freeport, Texas, who liked buying land with water frontage. Nicholson, an absentee landowner, had plans to develop the land, but meanwhile he leased it to local farmers and ranchers to grow crops and graze livestock.

A Cool Party Place

By the mid-1960s word had spread that a lovely, unattended swimming hole not far west of Austin was a cool party place. It was truly cool because during the Hill Country summers the temperature in the cypress-shaded canyon with a spring-fed stream could be ten degrees lower than on the river or the dry plateau above.

It also was free. Hamilton Pool on the east side of the Pedernales was on private land and open to the public for a fee of one dollar a car. But only a mile away, on the other side of the river, you could just walk right in to paradise. At first, just a few began to visit, swearing friends to secrecy. One admirer was Marcia Ball, who would go on to become a Grammy-nominated blues singer and pianist. She arrived in Austin from Louisiana in April 1970:

> Our friends took us to Lake Travis and to Westcave when we were still thinking we were on our way to San Francisco. Those beautiful spots, in a wet spring, were amazing to me and were a big part of why we stayed in Austin. Westcave was one of those special places we would take our friends who were visiting, a little secret Shangri La.
>
> We parked just off the road where it widened out after you crossed the Pedernales and stepped over the already pressed down barbed wire fence. You could pick up the trail right there and were immediately in a different world than the arid hills away from the little stream. When I went back recently, I felt it so strongly where the new trail from above intersects with the creek. I remember it being that lush all the way up.
>
> In 1971, there was a play called "Earl of Ruston" being rehearsed and previewed at the Armadillo [World Headquarters in Austin] and the band in the play were friends of ours from Baton Rouge, so we took them out there. It must have been in the late winter or very early spring because the guitar player, Bootsie Normand, jumped off the big rock into the pool in his long john union suit and the water was so cold his heart practically stopped. He was in and out in a second.
>
> We swam there some but never camped. One time we climbed up the cliff behind the caves to where the water fell and found a nest of snakes in a depression in the rocks. We left. Quickly.
>
> I guess we must have known it belonged to someone but we felt we weren't doing any harm. I'm so glad it has been preserved. It has a very special place in my heart.

Bill Brooks experienced his first free rappel at Heinz Branch canyon about 1970:

We parked near the river crossing and stayed on the right canyon wall. We walked to a spot where a large pointed rock overhangs the canyon. It was here we tied off, slipped over the edge, and rappelled to the floor of the canyon. We did this several times before walking up to the waterfall and scrambling through the little cave to the side of the falls. Yes, we soaked in the travertine pool on the near side of the pond. Our "guide" was a member of the University [of Texas] Speleological Society. I was told that these were the best and largest examples of travertine dams in the state. We were careful. About the time we were heading out of the canyon, the owner showed up. I was told he was

Marcia Ball and brother Van Mouton with friend Ronnie Bertrand at the Westcave grotto in 1970. Photo by Bob Ball, courtesy of Marcia Ball

carrying a shotgun. I never saw him but I sure heard a booming voice say, "Get off my property!" We complied.

Yvonne Baron Estes first snuck into the Westcave canyon during the summer of 1970, even though she had heard the owner might shoot trespassers. "My stupid friends and I were not deterred," she said:

> We entered the canyon the only way you could get in, by way of the river. We climbed the barbed wire fence and scrambled over all the rocks in the streambed. There were ferns everywhere, and even though it was summer, the canyon was lush and cool and unbelievably green. We had been to Hamilton Pool many times, and it was as if all the beauty of Hamilton Pool had been concentrated into this tiny unspoilt place. We could hear the waterfall long before we saw it, and then there it was, maidenhair fern everywhere, green on the canyon walls, green reflected in the pool. God, it was beautiful!
>
> At the time I was a graduate student at Cal Berkeley, and I knew the fern folks in the Botany Department. They were interested in my stories of Texas ferns. The next summer on my annual trip home I lugged a plant press with my collected specimens of *Cheilanthes alabamensis* (Alabama Lipfern) and other treasures. Yes, my name is on the identification labels of certain herbarium specimens at UC Berkeley. I'm going to hell.
>
> Some years later, after I wrote about Westcave for Third Coast Magazine, became a board member, and volunteered at the preserve, I confessed my fern collecting to John Ahrns, the resident manager. I was embarrassed, but John, ever generous, just laughed. He said, "Yes, and you've been expiating your sins ever since!"

The reminiscences of these three are the tip of the iceberg. Many longtime Austin residents either snuck into paradise in the early days or know someone who did.

Environmental awareness was strengthening in the 1960s and '70s, but the majority of visitors were young and had other things on their minds. Some chopped down trees for firewood, took travertine from the waterfall area and stalactites and stalagmites from the cave as souvenirs, and left their garbage behind. This was the era of sex, drugs, and rock 'n' roll, and this land was the botanical embodiment of that creed. The number of trespassers grew from a few people a week to several hundred. Sometimes there would be thirty or more cars parked at the crossing. This much use took a toll on the land, especially the fragile vegetation such as orchids and ferns, which were all but obliterated.

In 1974 a concerned John Covert Watson purchased the preserve's original twenty-five acres, including the canyon, grotto, and plateau above. Watson had been visiting Hamilton Pool since he was a boy, and he discovered the Westcave grotto in the early 1960s. After purchasing the land, Watson hired an on-site caretaker, John Ahrns, and together they dreamed and schemed about turning the land into an official nature preserve. The area was cleaned of trash, a small parking lot and single trail were established, and access was limited to guided tours only, setting in place the recovery of the natural gem that is Westcave Preserve.

Dwarf Palmetto (*Sabal minor*) in flower. Illustration by Nancy McGowan

13 ❧ THE JOHN AHRNS ERA, 1974–2010

He was born in the summer of his 27th year
coming home to a place he'd never been before.

—John Denver, "Rocky Mountain High," a song John Ahrns identified
with and played on his guitar

JOHN FREDRICK AHRNS
February 24, 1947–January 20, 2014
Texas Naturalist and Educator
Westcave Preserve Resident Manager, 1974–2010

Anyone with a multitude of nicknames is worth paying attention to. In 1974, when John Ahrns arrived at the land that would be named Westcave Preserve, wearing short shorts and with wild hair brushing his shoulders, he was dubbed Hippie John and Trapper John by the locals. His son Jeff's friends called him Grizzly Ahrns, after the then popular television series *Grizzly Adams*. He was Big Daddy, due to his willingness to help neighbors with practical problems. That, plus his outgoing personality and his stewardship of the area's first nature preserve, made him the de facto mayor of the Hammetts Crossing area. The ground rules for preserving the land were strictly enforced (always with a charming smile), so he came to be called The Law West of the Pedernales. He was such a skilled enforcer that his colleagues at Hamilton Pool Preserve across the river called him Mad Dog. As the neighbors got to know and appreciate him, they called him Our Hippie, and as his tenure at Westcave Preserve grew into decades and his fame as a naturalist and educator spread, Ahrns was called the Johnny Appleseed of Hamilton Pool Road—high praise, indeed.

Ahrns grew up in northwest Dallas near Bachman Lake, hunting, fly fishing, exploring alleys, and collecting rocks. He spent summers on camping trips with his mother, Ann, and sister, Anita. That, plus Boy Scout adventures and volunteering in parks, was a precursor of what was to come. He later admitted that in his unruly childhood he had "outraged nature, shot turtles, broke off tree limbs, you name it," but "from the time I was ten years old and saw my first Park Service Ranger with his Smoky the Bear hat on, I said that's what I want to be." In the early 1960s he read *The Web of Life: A First Book of Ecology*, by John H. Storer, and was smitten by how everything is connected. Later, it was the book he would always recommend.

John Ahrns. Ahrns family photo

At age twenty-seven his checkered career of working at various jobs while attending college but never earning a degree was about to come together at the best university any naturalist could hope for. Ahrns had gone to school with the daughter of Edward (Ned) Fritz, a Dallas attorney who was one of the founders of The Nature Conservancy of Texas, and later considered to be the father of Texas conservation. Ahrns and Fritz had become hiking buddies, so in 1974 when Fritz heard from John Covert Watson in Austin that Watson had just bought twenty-five acres in western Travis County and needed a resident land manager, Fritz put Ahrns and Watson together.

The reason Watson needed an on-site manager was the same reason the previous owner,

John Ahrns in his Cub Scout uniform in Dallas. Ahrns family photo

John Covert Watson: Westcave Preserve's Founding Father

The man who would become its savior first set eyes on what would become Westcave Preserve in the early 1960s as one of the early trespassers. John Covert Watson, from an old Austin family, had long visited nearby Hamilton Pool. But when he was about thirty years old, he heard rumors of another swimming hole nearby. "So I did what I fought against years later—I trespassed on the land," said Watson. Along with two adventuresome friends, Watson climbed over an old barbed wire fence and found a trail leading into a canyon. The threesome encountered a group just exiting who warned of snakes and poison ivy. Undaunted, they followed the trail along a flowing creek, through towering Bald Cypress trees and blooming Columbines, lured by the distant sound of falling water. Watson still remembers finding "the most splendid verdant grotto with Maidenhair Fern, a stunning waterfall, a pond, and a seductive cave to be explored."

Enchanted by his find, Watson continued to trespass, bringing friends and family. One day, a For Sale sign on the property stopped him in his tracks. Already he was concerned by the continuing abuse of this natural gem. But it was more than that. He was a specialist in organically designed homes in which everything relates to the surrounding environment, and experiencing this self-contained world had begun to inspire and reinforce his architectural juices.

John Covert Watson, Westcave founding father. Photo by Nancy Scanlan

Beginning in 1954, Watson had apprenticed with the renowned Frank Lloyd Wright, who was known for his philosophy of designing structures in harmony with nature. Watson went first to Wright's winter headquarters, Taliesin West, in Scottsdale, Arizona, and then to Taliesin in Spring Green, Wisconsin. After Taliesen, Watson worked in San Francisco for Wright's representative on the West Coast, Aaron Green. During that period Green's office was implementing the Wright-designed Marin County Civic Center in San Rafael, California, which is now a national- and state-designated historic landmark.

His experiences in the 1950s helped shape Watson's love affair with the architecture of the grotto area in the 1960s. "Westcave really transformed my architectural life because it is a great example of scale and proportion," said Watson. "It all seems to fit. It's all the way it's supposed to be. There was something in the detail that captured your eye."

Watson describes Hamilton Pool as Roman—on a grand scale—and Westcave Preserve's grotto as more Grecian—smaller and feminine. He also observed and learned from the light and shadows on the two grottos and how the day starts and ends at both, noting how different they are because Westcave's waterfall is at the west end of a short canyon, and Hamilton Pool's is at the east end of its canyon.

Westcave's grotto had become not only a place of recreation for Watson, but also "filled a great void in my architectural life." In one fell swoop Watson would leave trespassing behind and become the visionary conservationist. In 1974 he purchased the twenty-five acres containing his favorite grotto with money willed to him by Marjorie Watson, his aunt. The two of them had visited this special place together and had gone on many outdoor adventures in Colorado. "She was a great birder and appreciated all of nature's wonders," said Watson. "I feel certain she would have approved of my use of her gift."

In a whirlwind two years, Watson considered and dismissed the idea of building modest structures on the bluff overlooking the river for use by family and friends. What was needed was immediate control of the land, so Watson hired John Ahrns, who became the resident manager, to clean the site and deal with trespassers. Watson purchased a mobile home for the Ahrns family, placing it in a prominent position to protect access to the land.

The two Johns grew close, walking the property and talking about its future as an educational site and a dedicated natural area, both of which Ahrns advocated. All the while, Watson and other friends had been discussing the site's long-term protection, structured in such a way that the public might continue to visit. These discussions culminated in the establishment of the Westcave Preserve Corporation in 1976. The nonprofit cemented the concepts of permanent protection, careful restoration, and prudent visitor control. In 1983, after expenses at the preserve had exceeded revenue for several years, Watson brought to fruition a partnership with the Lower Colorado River Authority, which paid off the note and simultaneously conveyed management authority back to Westcave Preserve Corporation with a ninety-nine-year lease at one dollar per year.

To honor its founding father, in 2008 Westcave Preserve created the annual John Covert Watson Award for Vision, given at its annual celebration. Also, the preserve's main trail is now named John Covert Watson Canyon Trail.

"It was a labor of love," said Watson. "It really was one of the most pleasurable arcs in my life, and a good association with interesting people along the way."

W. D. Nicholson, had put the land up for sale: those pesky trespassers. Ahrns and his wife, Brenda, came for an interview with Watson, bringing Jeff, five, but leaving Amber, two, in Dallas. They walked with Watson and attorney Alfred Glenn down to the grotto, and Brenda remembers Jeff "running around, asking questions about everything." The young couple was impressed by the land's beauty and agreed there was "so much potential." In March 1974 Ahrns borrowed a friend's bus and moved his family to the middle of nowhere to manage what would become Westcave Preserve. "I just moved us to heaven," he told a visitor later. "I still think of it as the chance of a lifetime."

The heart of heaven was a quarter-mile, creek-cut canyon that had been loved almost to death by a decade's worth of trespassers. Watson and his friends already had started to clean the canyon, hauling out countless bags of human waste and trash. Once they arrived, Ahrns and his Dallas friend Frank Harrison, plus a handful of volunteers, completed the job, dragging hundreds of trash bags full of bottles, beer cans, glass, charcoal, broken lanterns, plastic, and paper out of the canyon. They scraped mud off the floor of the fragile cave. They took sand from near the waterfall to cover and begin the healing process of the ground that had been sterilized by campfires. Ahrns erased most of the cave's graffiti by applying water and letting the rock moss grow over it.

Jeff, Brenda, John, and Amber Ahrns at Westcave Preserve in 1979. The visitor center now occupies the bluebonnet field behind them. Ahrns family photo

The easy part over, they beheld a wasteland where the Bald Cypress trees still stood, but the understory bushes, ferns, and orchids that had once made this a lush box canyon had been stripped and the soil compressed by thousands of tramping feet. Trees had been felled for firewood. Experts advised that, left to its own devices, the land would heal itself. This became Ahrns's mantra and the guiding philosophy for the preserve: "If you leave things alone, they will recover."

Another part of the job was keeping trespassers out, which Ahrns was surprised to learn could be dangerous. Watson equipped Ahrns and Harrison, who stayed a few months, with walkie-talkies to make them look more official and saw the irony in asking hippies to police the largely hippie interlopers. Brenda remembers that she and Ahrns and Harrison spent many hours sitting near the mouth of the creek where it flowed into the Pedernales, the trespassers' favored entry point to the canyon Shangri-La, yelling at people to turn around.

"I didn't even consider that it might be dangerous," Ahrns told Max Woodfin of the *Austin American-Statesman* in 1982, but after he'd been cursed and threatened with fists, knives, guns, and even one of the preserve's own stalactites, Ahrns was glad he stood over six feet tall. "People complain that we have ruined a good thing here. They actually get mad that they can't come in and trash the place," said Ahrns.

The situation was so bad that, for about three years, not only was law enforcement called often to evict the outraged trespassers, but the county judge offered, according to Watson, to "hold court right here" on the weekends, just to cope with the overwhelming number of violators. That never happened, but Ahrns did become the de facto Law West of the Pedernales, a reference to the infamous Judge Roy Bean who in the late 1800s called himself the Law West of the Pecos and held court in Langtry in southwest Texas.

The Ahrns plan was to offer guided tours to the exquisite waterfall and emerald pool at the head of the canyon. A single trail needed to be built to minimize destruction. With Brenda away at work and Jeff at school, Ahrns would bring baby Amber with him to the part of the trail he was working on that day, set her up on a blanket with her toys, and go to work.

This is the trail that is still the only way in and out of the canyon, with its 125 uneven steps transporting the hiker from a more moderate ecosystem below, through a limestone aquifer, and to the drier plateau above. Ahrns spent many days, using only hand tools, building both cement and wooden steps, depending on the terrain, and securing posts before stringing cable handrails. Ahrns worked on fences, especially near Hammetts Crossing, which was the way trespassers had gained entry to the box canyon. He also removed nonnative plants and some Ashe Juniper, which had become invasive in the more heavily damaged parts of the property. To reintroduce species that had been extinguished by overzealous visitors, Ahrns also planted trees and collected plants, starting some from seed. Brenda remembers that Ahrns babied some plants, watering them every day.

At first, Brenda remembers, Ahrns led five public tours a day on the weekends—at 10 am, 12 noon, and 2, 4, and 6 pm. She soon convinced him that that was too much, and he ended the 6 pm tours. Interestingly, weekend tours at 10, 12, 2, and 4 are still the norm. The tours were free, but there was a metal donation box, chained to a post, at the top of the trail.

Neighborhood Headquarters

Almost immediately after the family's arrival, Ahrns put a chair under a tree near the single-wide trailer that John Watson had provided for the resident manager's family, and that became the preserve headquarters. Over time that spot also would become the neighborhood headquarters, and Ahrns the area's cornerstone. "Back in the old days, everybody came by and introduced themselves, you know, I'm so and so, I live down the road," said Ahrns. "I have this desire to communicate with everybody. Generally, I give people about ten times more information than they really wanted to know!" If neighbors needed area news, they knew where to come.

He didn't dress like his neighbors, and his politics might not have matched theirs, but with his striking blue eyes, high-pitched chuckles, and exceptional smile, he proved himself to be generous, brutally honest, and

The Ahrns firepit was the neighborhood gathering place. From left, Ann Ahrns (John's mother), Ralph Combest, Brenda Ahrns, Ellen Lain, Keith Lain (behind Ellen), Randy and Sharon Barton, and John Ahrns. Ahrns family photo

a man of principle and honor. He also was a good worker—"unbridled energy in a human body," as his friend Dan Chapman said at Ahrns's memorial service. He helped many neighbors build outbuildings or herd cattle and fix fences. He offered a ride when needed or a jump start when a vehicle battery went dead. He wanted company on his trips into town and always invited someone to ride with him. He saved a woman clinging to a tree during a flood on nearby Cypress Creek. He saved two teenagers on flooded Hamilton Creek by tying himself to his truck with a rope and going into the water to save them. He was always in the neighborhood, so always on call, happy to help with anything.

He also was a good listener, a natural storyteller, and a self-taught guitar and piano player of considerable talent who enjoyed playing host and sharing the family fire pit. Neighbors recall many evenings filled with song when they brought a potluck dish and stood or sat around the fire. Many came out of curiosity and were soon friends, their kids knowing each other from the schools in Dripping Springs.

Loretta Cook remembers that Ahrns made it a point to spend time with her father Alton Oscar Kneese, who owned the AOK Ranch three miles west of the preserve, after her father got older and more housebound. Area residents would gather at each others' homes for an annual Christmas party, featuring white elephant gifts that are still talked about. Croquet was played at neighbors' homes, and memorable chili cook-offs were held at the home of Mike Kelley.

Ahrns struck up a special friendship with retired colonel Peter Agnell, who owned land on the other side of the road from the preserve. The creek that drained to the Westcave waterfall and grotto passed first through Colonel Agnell's land. Ahrns and Agnell agreed on a conservation project that would benefit them both. The grotto was being destroyed by gravel carried off Colonel Agnell's land after heavy rains, filling the plunge pool below the waterfall and scouring everything on through the canyon. Colonel Agnell consulted the Texas Department of Agriculture, installed erosion barriers, and the situation improved. "He was our buddy and a good neighbor," said Watson.

Neighborhood Folklore: Incidents from the 1970s and 1980s

One of the worst accidents of this era took place on Friday, April 13, 1979, and involved neighbor Ralph Combest and John Ahrns's son Jeff, who was ten years old. Jeff was helping Combest build a house literally off the side of the cliff. The Pedernales River canyon is about sixty feet deep where they were working. Jeff was on the canyon rim, with Combest perched precariously on a boulder about forty feet away, just thin air between them. They were building a ladder across the gap, with Combest trying to cut a steel guy wire with a hacksaw, yanking on it to get it into place, when he lost his balance. "I watched him fall. I watched him hit the ground. It was surreal," said Jeff, who climbed down to find Combest twenty-five feet below with a mangled arm and bloody face. Warning Combest not to move, Jeff ran for help. Combest was in the hospital for days, and when he came home, the Ahrns family insisted he convalesce at their home. "His arm is still kind of mangled, but we ended up finishing his house. It's one-of-a-kind," said Jeff, who would go on to build several houses of his own.

One day in the late 1970s John Ahrns got in his yellow Chevy truck to cross the river and pick up mail at the boxes on the other side. He met neighbor Agnell, who invited Ahrns to join him. The river was about six inches over the low-water crossing, so Ahrns parked his truck in a place he thought was far enough upslope to be safe. On the other side, the two men spent time chatting with neighbors, and when they started back, the river had risen and they could not get across. So they drove the forty-mile roundabout way to get back to their side of the river, but by the time they reached the truck, only the antenna was visible. Word spread, and by the next day when the river went down, an amused group of neighbors showed up to see what was now being called the Yellow Submarine. Ahrns pulled open the door, and the truck was full of sand. Somehow, Ahrns got the truck running again.

More Neighbors

From 1976 to 1983, Shirley and Leonard Fehrle managed the 2,400-acre Hill Country Scout Ranch across the Pedernales River with their sons Leonard Jr. and Lance. Before Westcave Preserve had a telephone, the Ahrns family communicated with the Fehrles by means of a citizens band radio, and anyone wanting to telephone the Ahrnses was asked to call the Fehrles, who would pass on the message.

Other original neighbors included the Burleson, Myers, Reimers, and Stieler families. Gradually, the land along Hamilton Pool Road and Fearless Treadway to the west of the preserve, in Hammetts Crossing subdivision to the north, and in La Tierra to the south was bought and occupied. New neighbors included Sharon and Randy and Barton, Patti and David Boyd, Tricia and Floyd Davis, Ellen and Keith Lain, John McLaurin and daughter Amy, Loretta Royal, Ric Sternberg and Annie Borden, Anne and Charles Walton, and Felixa and Murray Walton and daughter Katie. Many of these friends and neighbors helped with repairs and reached into their own pocket to subsidize the preserve when the financial situation was shaky.

A community of neighbors had slowly developed in this rural area, brought together by its de facto mayor. It took a while, but eventually the locals began to call Ahrns "Our Hippie." Friends remember that, above all, Ahrns talked about his family and how much he loved them.

The Community Organizer and Educator

If Ahrns was everybody's best friend, he also was a community organizer before the job title was a job title. He looked in the phone book and found the Austin Nature & Science Center: "So I called them up, said 'What do you guys do?' They told me and I said, 'Well, we just started a preserve, let's work together.' And that was the first group I worked with." At that time,

Chris Caran was the center's supervisor, and the two became friends.

Ahrns traveled to schools in Dripping Springs, Johnson City, and Lake Travis, inviting teachers to bring students to Westcave Preserve to fulfill their natural science credits. These education programs would become his passion, and he developed various field trip options to enhance what students were learning at school. He proved to be a gifted teacher, just like his mother. "The trick is to educate, not indoctrinate," said Ahrns. "My first year, I was the Big Botanist. I quickly learned nobody cared about the Latin names." Instead, he developed "worthless plant tricks," using plants as attention-getters. He would hold up a Roughleaf Dogwood leaf, split it in half, and say he was going to make half of the leaf disappear: "It has this sinewy stuff in the leaves and from a distance, it'll look like I made it disappear. And then I start talking about the vascular system. Now, if I talked about the vascular system, it would have gone in one ear and out the other, but they'll remember the worthless plant trick."

Ahrns kept and valued every thank you note he received. "Dear John, Thank you for inviting our class and telling us about the Westcave Preserve. I learned that Texas has 5,000 kinds of flowers. The best part I like [sic] was the stalactites. Love, Justin." And another: "Dear John, Thank you for Shoing [sic] us arend [sic] Westcave and my favorite port [sic] was the cave

"The trick is to educate, not indoctrinate," said John Ahrns, shown practicing his passionate pursuit of environmental education. Source unknown

and most of all I wanted to tell you thank you for being are [sic] tour guide. Your firend [sic] Ben." Some of those kids are now bringing their own children and grandchildren to visit Westcave Preserve.

Ahrns welcomed and sought out scientists and researchers to study the property, which, as it healed, turned out to be exceptionally diverse, with several distinct habitats. He went to numerous parks and museums to study the way they operated. He spent countless hours at the Austin History Center, researching the Hammetts Crossing area. "I mooched an education, is what I did," said Ahrns. "Doctor so and so came out and he'd answer a stupid question because I asked him. I've had the opportunity to work with some really brilliant people."

Over the years Ahrns made it a point to get to know every park, natural area, stream, valley, swimming hole, and back road in central Texas. He also traveled more widely, taking backpacking trips in the American West with family and friends. On his days off, Ahrns worked at Pedernales Falls State Park, the Lyndon B. Johnson National Historical Park (LBJ Ranch) near Stonewall, and the LBJ Boyhood Home in Johnson City. He also was a substitute teacher in Dripping Springs.

Ahrns volunteered for Texas Parks and Wildlife Department, Travis County Parks, Wild Basin Wilderness Preserve, Austin Nature & Science Center, Lady Bird Johnson Wildflower Center, Bamberger Ranch Preserve, and Selah. He was a popular guest speaker for local groups and for classes at St. Edward's University, the University of Texas at Austin, and Austin Community College. "He did these things out of joy for nature and the thrill of sharing his knowledge," said Brenda.

His phenomenal memory, insatiable curiosity, and eager need to talk to anyone about everything served him well, and he became a "self-taught nature genius," according to Lee Walker, Westcave's board chair for twenty-eight years. "John would see stuff and hear stuff that we mere mortals would not. And then he had this extraordinary memory and could name that which he had noticed. In a half hour you might move 10 feet, because there was just so much going on." Watson, the man who hired Ahrns in 1974 and thought of him more as a family member than an employee, admired Ahrns's curiosity about everything. "His greatest asset was that he could not seem to have enough information about anything," said Watson. "But he was smart enough to know who to listen to."

Part of the Ahrns philosophy was: "We're not teachers. We're here to interpret what's here and then when you go home, hopefully it will have tweaked your interest a little bit in the geology or the bird you heard or that

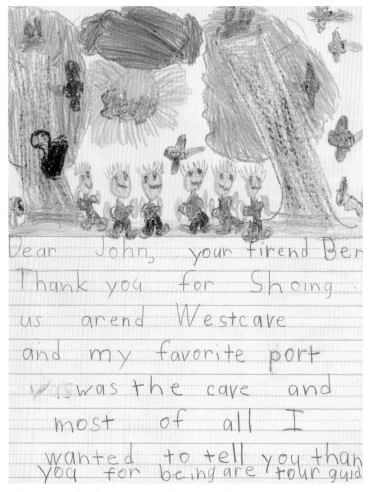

Thank you note from Ben to John Ahrns after a school field trip.
Westcave Archives

butterfly landing on that plant or that bug. You know, this is their house, we're just visitors."

Westcave Preserve Corporation and Partnering with the LCRA

All the while, the business of the preserve went on, with Ahrns involved in every detail. In 1975 Watson's friend Alfred Glenn had purchased five acres just north of Watson's land and upstream from the waterfall and grotto. This parcel would act as a buffer to protect the fragile canyon below. In 1976

Glenn's five acres and Watson's twenty-five acres were purchased by the nonprofit Westcave Preserve Corporation, cementing the concepts of permanent protection, careful restoration, and prudent visitor control.

John Ahrns (left) and John Covert Watson in 1995. Photo by Nancy Scanlan

In 1983 Westcave Preserve partnered with the LCRA, which cited Ahrns's dedication to and management of the preserve among the reasons for buying the property, then leasing it back to the Westcave Preserve Corporation at one dollar a year for ninety-nine years. The nonprofit corporation maintained management authority to sustain the preserve and offer it as an educational resource.

The chair-under-the-tree visitor center was upgraded with a storage shed and then augmented by a used fireworks stand. In 1990 the stand was replaced with a double-wide trailer. At last there was a place for events and exhibits and for visiting graduate students to spend a few days.

In 1996 Westcave Preserve was incorporated into the Balcones Canyonlands Preserve (BCP) system, widely studied as a model for public-private partnership. The BCP comprises over 30,500 acres scattered throughout western Travis County. Under given circumstances, developers wishing to build in environmentally sensitive areas may avoid prolonged and expensive environmental surveys and administrative procedures by providing mitigation funds used to expand the BCP. The approach balances the

Amber Ahrns volunteered at the Lyndon B. Johnson National Historical Park, boyhood home of the former president in Johnson City, Texas, where her father John worked part-time. Ahrns family photo

protection of endangered species habitat with economic development in one of the most rapidly developing areas in the United States.

In 1997, a plan was launched to build what would become a world-class three-thousand-square-foot model of sustainable building design to serve as visitor center, classroom space, living science laboratory, and natural history museum. Lee Walker was one of the guiding forces behind the capital improvements project *Nurturing the Land, Building for the Future* that would result in the dedication in 2003 of the $1.7 million Environmental Learning Center.

From the time he first set eyes on the preserve in 1978, Walker became one of its strongest allies. He led tours when Ahrns was away and soon joined the board, becoming president in 1980. He retained that position until 2008 and was named chair emeritus. Walker said that the guiding force behind the new building project was not only to develop a state-of-the-art learning center but also to provide better housing for John and Brenda Ahrns, whose children had moved out by that time. Since the Ahrns family had arrived in 1974, they had lived in a single-wide trailer, which had undergone various improvements, including a large wooden carport-style structure that the LCRA built over the trailer to protect it from rain and sun.

Walker said that when he began seeking donors for improving the residence, there were no takers. So Walker and the board asked what would change a "no" to a "yes," and the idea of a nature center came up, which could, of course, include a residence. "I was reminded of that old saying that sometimes the obstacle is the way," said Walker. Walker's connections led to the first large donation, one hundred thousand dollars, from the Warren Skaaren Foundation. Skaaren, one of Hollywood's top screenwriters, had died a few years before, and Amon Burton from the Skaaren Foundation pledged that amount to kick start the funding. "It was truly a large community of public and private donors that came together, shoulder to shoulder, to imagine this and find the funding," said Walker. Other funding partners included the LCRA, Texas Parks and Wildlife Department, Lee

From 1990 until 2003, a double-wide trailer served as the preserve's visitor center. Ahrns family photo

Walker and Jennifer Vickers, and the Betty Norsworthy family. Ahrns helped oversee the design and construction of what was named the Warren Skaaren Environmental Learning Center, which included a separate space for offices and a residence.

In 2005, Westcave Preserve hired Executive Director and CEO Molly Stevens, who had been Texas regional managing director for The Environmental Defense Fund and before that development director for The Nature Conservancy of Texas. In 2008 the preserve acquired an additional forty-five acres of land known as the Uplands. This parcel is upsteam from the waterfall and grotto and protects the quality and quantity of spring water that feeds them. Also in 2008, Westcave Preserve created the John F. Ahrns Award for Environmental Education, presented at its annual Celebration of Children and Nature, to recognize exemplary natural science educators in the community.

Ahrns Farewell

In 2010, after thirty-seven years, Ahrns retired. The occasion was marked by the dedication of the limestone Ahrns Bench at the top of the trail leading into the canyon. To honor the entire family, native trees were planted in the Ahrns Grove at the entrance to the Uplands.

Ahrns died of cancer in 2014 at age sixty-six. There was standing room only at his memorial service. Music by James Horner from the title track of Ahrns's favorite movie, Star Trek II: The Wrath of Khan, boomed out over the crowd. One thing heard again and again was how much the preserve meant to those assembled, but that it was not just the place that kept people coming back. A big part of the attraction was the magnetism of the man with the many nicknames.

When Ahrns retired in 2010, he was asked about his legacy. "I want to be remembered for nothing in particular," he said. "I'm just lucky to be here and do a job I like. I've plagiarized, asked too many damn questions and had lots of help. I've done nothing special." Nothing, that is, except be the expert and passionate guardian of a nature preserve, help inspire the creation of two adjacent public parks from what had been private property (Hamilton Pool Preserve in 1985 and Milton Reimers Ranch Park in 2006), and touch the lives of hundreds of thousands of established and budding naturalists—high praise, indeed, Mr. Johnny Appleseed of Hamilton Pool Road.

Ahrns, by the way, who was not one to seek the limelight, would have hated that last paragraph.

Lee Walker: *Westcave Preserve's Board Chair, 1980–2008*

Lee Walker visited Westcave Preserve for the first time in 1978 on the advice of a clerk at an Austin convenience store who said it was the most beautiful place on Earth. Walker had fallen in love with nature as a boy splashing in a creek behind his home in Three Rivers, Texas. He was back in the state after getting his MBA at Harvard University, then launching and selling a handful of successful start-up companies.

From the time he had first come to Austin, as a boy playing basketball in University Interscholastic League tournaments, Walker knew he would come to live in the capital of Texas one day. Twenty-five years later, he made the move, relieved to put behind him a decade of cold winters in the Northeast. "I felt a terrible sense of disorientation, and was looking for something," he said. Just one visit to the preserve and a talk with resident manager John Ahrns produced "a very strong feeling that bonded me with Westcave," Walker remembers.

He would come back often and go on many exploratory walks with Ahrns. The two visited dozens of regional natural areas together. Walker liked making notes in a little blue book, which he still has. When Ahrns took the occasional vacation, Walker would step in as the preserve's weekend guide. He has said that just being at the preserve and having Ahrns as a friend saved him at that point in his life.

Walker joined Westcave Preserve's board and became its chairman in 1980. On his twenty-seven-year watch, the preserve partnered with the Lower Colorado River Authority, which bought the property in 1983 and leased it back to the Westcave Preserve Corporation at one dollar a year for ninety-nine years. Walker was one of the guiding forces behind the 1997 capital improvements project, *Nurturing the Land, Building for the Future* that resulted in the dedication in 2003 of the $1.7 million Warren Skaaren Environmental Learning Center.

Lee Walker, Westcave board chairman, 1980–2008. Photo by Nancy Scanlan

As Walker contemplated his retirement from the board, he recognized that the preserve needed an experienced leader for an expanded mission in the twenty-first century. In 2005 Walker led the board in hiring Molly Stevens as CEO. In 2008 Stevens and Walker worked under the leadership of new Board Chair Max Scoular to double the preserve's physical footprint by acquiring the forty-five-acre Uplands property.

In 2009 Stevens led the development of the Children in Nature Collaborative of Austin, which later became incorporated as a core program of Westcave. She and the Westcave staff also have worked in partnership with the Shield Ranch and El Buen Samaritano Episcopal Mission to create El Ranchito summer camp. With this growth came the need to better represent the organization's wider range of programs by adopting a new name, Westcave Outdoor Discovery Center.

All the while, Walker was making his mark in Austin, where he was the first president of Dell Computer Corporation, chaired the board of directors for Capital Metro from 1997 to 2008, and became a Senior Research Fellow at the Plan II Honors Program at the University of Texas. He was named Austinite of the Year by the Austin Chamber of Commerce in 1997, served as president of the Livestrong Foundation during its early heyday, helped lead the successful Save Our Springs campaign in 1992, and in 2006 received the Lifetime Achievement Award from The Nature Conservancy of Texas.

If Walker was saved by Westcave Preserve, he in turn saved the preserve time and time again. He served as its chief volunteer officer and primary benefactor for almost thirty years. His leadership and support were and are vital components of Westcave's history and key contributors to its success.

14 🌿 GROWING UP AT WESTCAVE PRESERVE

Amber Ahrns Gosselin

In 1974, John and Brenda Ahrns became the first resident managers at Westcave Preserve. Their daughter, Amber, was two years old, and her brother, Jeff, was five. This is Amber's remembrance of her growing up.

"Go outside and find something to do!" Those are the words my brother Jeff and I heard countless times in our youth. My parents had many "famous" sayings, and that was one we heard in the summer, on a regular basis—usually from my dad. My mom's favorite was "Watch out for snakes!"

I don't have any earlier memories than those at Westcave Preserve. We moved there when I was two and my brother was five. Lucky for us, my father, John Ahrns, accepted a job to take care of some land and run off the trespassers. This move would dramatically change the trajectory of our whole family.

Our lives would have been so different if we had stayed in Dallas. When we moved to the "sticks," there was no phone, no water, a single-wide trailer, and twenty-five amazing acres. Those Hill Country acres may not have seemed so amazing when we got there, but we all know better now. After all, as a teenager, wouldn't it have been better to live somewhere that the pizza places delivered to, or, better yet, have a mall and movie theater close by?

It wasn't until college that I began to realize how unique my childhood was. Don't get me wrong. I realized that none of my friends grew up on a nature preserve, used an outhouse (at least until we got a real toilet), or had a father who was constantly in a magazine or news story. College friends would ask, "What was it like to grow up at Westcave?" or "Is your dad really John Ahrns?" or "You must have just loved growing up in a nature preserve!" Reflecting back as an adult, I now realize it was an extraordinary

Amber Ahrns cruising through the Westcave gate at age nine. Ahrns family photo

childhood. Nobody I have ever met had a childhood like mine. That single-wide trailer, those twenty-five acres, those parents, brother, neighbors, community—there is just no comparison. Lucky me!

Finding something outside to do was easier than we realized. We had access not only to the preserve but to land owned by our neighbors—Colonel Agnell and the Nicholsons, among others. We would hike all over, pick through trash piles from the 1950s to find "treasures," and create cool forts (at least six that I can remember) to save us from boredom.

Every summer my cousins Gary and Dana would come from Dallas to stay. We loved having that time together. Epic kickball games and crazy tag/jail/hide-and-go-seek games had us running barefoot for hours until it was dark and mom called us for dinner. We would collect T-shirts full of Texas Persimmon berries and have wars flinging them at each other. The ripe black ones would stain your shirt, and the unripe green ones would sting if you got tagged. I became a semipro at this sport, but, unfortunately for me, my brother was a pro. Speargrass throwing was another fun, try-and-hurt-your-sibling game. We went to sleep to the sound of the box fan humming in the window.

On hot summer days we'd beg mom to take us to the river. We'd spend hours on the water, sometimes with inner tubes but most times jumping off the rope on the Scout Ranch side. I was sure a creepy snake was waiting for me as I hurriedly climbed up the gnarled, worn cypress roots to get to the rope. I can remember all those other awesome swimming holes that my parents took us to on the Scout Ranch, Roy Creek, and Cypress Creek. These swimming holes are some of the prettiest I have ever seen, but they were just part of our normal backyard. Again, lucky me!

Living so far from a city, we neighbors all depended on each other for lots of things, but mostly companionship and entertainment. My family and some others were the transplants, but there were families who had been there for generations. At our parties my parents would have a big fire, and music was always playing and people were laughing. I can still see the sparks and embers flying in the dark and smell the burning wood. What an amazing neighborhood group we had—our extended family. We all took care of one another, enjoyed each other, and created a really tight community.

The flooding Pedernales River was always a neighborhood social event. There is something about that earthy, rotting vegetation smell that brings me back to being a kid and walking down to check on the river. All of the neighbors also would be checking on the river and catching up with one another. One time, Lake Travis had backed up into the river for weeks, so it was flooded and completely unpassable on foot or by car. The river was wide and calm. So dad would canoe across and pick everyone's mail up on the other side. He also canoed me across so my best friend, Moon, could pick me up and we could go out. Everyone thought it was so cool to cross in the canoe, but I just wanted to not be stuck at home and bored.

My dad was a very talented, self-taught musician. I have fond memories of him always playing his guitar or the piano, singing songs by Bob Dylan, Neil Young, and the Rolling Stones. I had no idea those songs weren't his songs. I'd hear them on the radio and think, "They've stolen my dad's song!" When I told him this, he'd just laugh with that ever-present twinkle in his clear-as-the-sky blue eyes.

Another common activity in the Ahrns family was looking for arrowheads. Jeff and dad would search all over the neighborhood. I found it terribly boring, but I'd tag along and pretend to be interested. The three of us would also have nightly games of basketball. We'd play HORSE or Around the World and every once in a while they'd let me win.

Of course, I wanted to do everything Jeff did, even though he was three and a half years older and a boy. I didn't care! If he was going to hunt, so would I. My dad let me hunt for the first time when I was twelve. He set me up on the Nicholson place with a .243 Remington with a scope on it. He presumably left, and then came back when he heard the gunshot. He went over to the deer and said, "Perfect shot, Amber. But you killed Bambi." I responded: "I didn't see the spots in the scope!" He laughed, but that was my one and only time to hunt. I still feel bad about that.

Luckily, my dad and brother still hunted because venison was a staple at our house—along with those darned veggies from our garden that we had to incessantly weed and harvest. Even that was much better than having "compost duty"!

My first paying job was at Westcave Preserve. Dad would pay Jeff or me ten dollars a day to greet visitors and get them ready for the next tour. We also closed the gate between tours, as dad was the only guide. I really didn't like doing it, but I enjoyed those ten dollars. I felt a bit timid meeting new people who were driving in from all over. But looking back, it was character-building—much like that compost pile.

We had a javelina named Spunky. I have no idea why or for how long, but we loved him. I can remember going to his pen and feeding him. He had massive teeth, stunk, and was spikey. He had a particular grunt about him that made me feel he was pleased to see me.

For a time, we also had rabbits. My brother and a neighbor friend, Lance, locked me in the rabbit hutch once because I wouldn't leave them alone. Mom rescued me. I guess they had had enough pestering from an annoying girl.

There was also a turkey that would chase Jeff and me. I can remember walking down our drive to the school bus stop or walking home and keeping a watchful/frightened eye out for the devil turkey. I was chased on many occasions, and Jeff, too. We told dad and he just said, "Stop messing with it and it will leave you alone." Of course, when the turkey finally chased my dad, that was the end of the turkey.

One constant we always had was a Great Pyrenees dog. We brought Nikki with us from Dallas. He was one year older than me and died when I was thirteen. There were others afterwards, but Nikki always had my heart—old, sweet, protective dog that he was.

As a child I can remember wanting to pick flowers, especially for my mom. I loved all the brilliant colors and smelling their sweet perfume. She'd put them in a pretty little blue vase and tell me how happy they made her. But my dad wouldn't let me pick a flower until I could tell him its name. I am not sure if he was trying to make me a naturalist or just instilling respect for nature, but both are now true.

I can recall one day when the waterfall had almost frozen. Dad dragged me down to the grotto to show me the huge icicles. It was incredible, even

Amber and Brenda Ahrns and Nikki on the porch at their Westcave Preserve home, 1976. Ahrns family photo

though I deliberately rolled my eyes several times when he was looking at me. But I was glad that he made me do this as well as many other things on the preserve. Those experiences have kept me curious about nature ever since.

When I got older I worked at Hamilton Pool Preserve for the better part of a decade. That is when I realized my childhood had prepared me for my soon-to-be career. Dad and I would always compete: two neighboring nature preserves, a father/daughter duo, same work ethic and love of nature. It was constant and fun. Who would hear the first Golden-cheeked Warbler of the season? Who would see the Chatterbox Orchid blooming first? Dad would tell me his Green Dragons were blooming, and I could never get to the ones at Hamilton Pool in time to see them bloom. He would always win that one—much to his excitement and delight.

I wanted to learn every plant, every animal, and the way everything worked so I could be like my dad. I went on to become a biologist for Travis County, managing large tracts of the Balcones Canyonlands Preserve. And the competition continued.

When I had my first baby girl, I went into semiretirement. After my second girl came along, I was offered the land manager position at Westcave Preserve. With great humility, I accepted. Could I do what my dad did—fill his shoes and carry on his legacy? Well, it remains to be seen. But I'm giving it the ole Ahrns try!

CONCLUSION

Preserving the Future of Westcave

Westcave Outdoor Discovery Center has been a respected proponent of conservation and stewardship for forty years and will continue to lead by example. Its success has come from salvaging, nurturing, and interpreting the area's environmental heritage and advocating for the rights of children to play and learn in nature.

The Westcave board, staff, and members look to the future, determined to promote environmental education, nature play, and conservation while motivating the environmentalists of tomorrow. The preserve is and will remain a touchstone of natural resource protection and inspiration.

Guadalupe Spiny Softshell turtle (*Apalone spinifera guadalupensis*) coming up for air. Illustration by Nancy McGowan

APPENDIXES
Species Lists

Scrub Live Oak (*Quercus fusiformis*) with acorns.
Illustration by Nancy McGowan

APPENDIX A

Plant Communities

S. Christopher Caran, Nan Hampton, and Bob Fulginiti

This list includes a representative selection of plant species (and some sub-species and varieties) found in each of the major habitats within Westcave Preserve and its immediate vicinity. Although these plants are common, they are particularly or uniquely adapted to only one or two specific habi-tats. Other plants that occupy numerous habitats, including some of the most common vines, grasses, and herbaceous wildflowers, are listed only in the habitat or habitats where they are most conspicuous.

In each habitat, trees (T) and shrubs (S) are listed first (in approximate descending order with respect to frequency), then vines (V), herbs (H), grasses (G), ferns and fern allies (F), mosses (M), and lichens (L).

Scientific names were checked against the United States Department of Agriculture's PLANTS Database (http://plants.usda.gov/) and/or the Integrated Taxonomic Information System (ITIS, http://www.itis.gov/index .html) and were current as of August 2015.

For a comprehensive inventory of the plants of Westcave Preserve, see the plant list in Appendix B.

Uplands

Plateau; flat upland areas

Scrub Live Oak (*Quercus fusiformis*) T
Ashe Juniper [cedar] (*Juniperus ashei*) T
Cedar Elm (*Ulmus crassifolia*) T
Netleaf Hackberry (*Celtis laevigata* var. *reticulata*) T
Post Oak (*Quercus stellata*) T
Texas Persimmon [Mexican Persimmon] (*Diospyros texana*) T/S
Honey Mesquite (*Prosopis glandulosa*) T/S

Texas Ash (*Fraxinus albicans*) T/S
Evergreen Sumac (*Rhus virens*) S
Prairie Flameleaf Sumac (*Rhus lanceolata*) S
Agarita [Agarito] (*Mahonia trifoliolata*) S
Possumhaw [Deciduous Holly] (*Ilex decidua*) S
Lotebush (*Ziziphus obtusifolia*) S
Texas Prickly Pear [Lindheimer Prickly Pear] (*Opuntia engelmannii var. lindheimeri*) S
Old Man's Beard (*Clematis drummondii*) V
Purple Passionflower (*Passiflora incarnata*) V
Pencil Cactus [Tasajillo, Christmas Cactus] (*Cylindropuntia leptocaulis*) H/S
Claret Cup (*Echinocereus triglochidiatus*) H
Twisted-leaf Yucca (*Yucca rupicola*) H/S
Bluebonnet (*Lupinus texensis*) H
Goldenwave (*Coreopsis tinctoria*) H
Indian Blanket [Firewheel] (*Gaillardia pulchella*) H
Bracted Winecup (*Callirhoe involucrata*) H
Golden-eye Phlox (*Phlox roemeriana*) H
Texas Aster (*Symphyotrichum drummondii var. texanum*) H
Blackfoot Daisy (*Melampodium leucanthum*) H
Fluttermill [Missouri Primrose] (*Oenothera macrocarpa ssp. macrocarpa*) H
Texas Lantana (*Lantana urticoides*) H/S
Antelope Horns (*Asclepias asperula*) H
Orange Milkweed [Butterfly-weed] (*Asclepias tuberosa*) H
Bluebell Gentian (*Eustoma exaltatum ssp. russellianum*) H
Hairy Wedelia [Zexmenia] (*Wedelia acapulcensis var. hispida*) H
Maximilian Sunflower (*Helianthus maximiliani*) H
Prairie Larkspur [Carolina Larkspur] (*Delphinium carolinianum spp.*) H
Puccoon (*Lithospermum incisum*) H
Spring Coralroot (*Corallorhiza wisteriana*) H
Yellow Stonecrop (*Sedum nuttallianum*) H
Ball Moss (*Tillandsia recurvata*) H
Mistletoe (*Phoradendron tomentosum*) H
Little Bluestem (*Schizachyrium scoparium*) G
Indiangrass (*Sorghastrum nutans*) G
Sideoats Grama (*Bouteloua curtipendula*) G
Buffalo Grass (*Bouteloua dactyloides*) G
Leucodon Moss (*Leucodon julaceus*) M
Square Pleurochaete Moss (*Pleurochaete squarrosa*) M

Slope (exposed)

Canyon walls of the Pedernales River and lowermost Heinz Branch

Scrub Live Oak (*Quercus fusiformis*) T
Ashe Juniper [Cedar] (*Juniperus ashei*) T
Texas Persimmon [Mexican Persimmon] (*Diospyros texana*) T/S
Honey Mesquite (*Prosopis glandulosa*) T/S
Texas Kidneywood [Beebush] (*Eysenhardtia texana*) S
Catclaw (*Acacia roemeriana*) S
Catclaw Mimosa (*Mimosa aculeaticarpa var. biuncifera*) S
Mormon Tea [Clapweed] (*Ephedra antisyphilitica*) H/S
Texas Prickly Pear [Lindheimer Prickly Pear] (*Opuntia engelmannii var. lindheimeri*) S
Oreja de Raton [Mouse Ears] (*Bernardia myricifolia*) S
Claret Cup (*Echinocereus triglochidiatus*) H
Bush Croton [Shrub Croton] (*Croton fruticulosus*) H
Sacahuista [Texas Beargrass] (*Nolina texana*) H/S
Texas Sotol (*Dasylirion texanum*) H
Puccoon (*Lithospermum incisum*) H
Prairie Goldenrod [Gray Goldenrod] (*Solidago nemoralis*) H
Jamaican Weissia Moss (*Weissia jamaicensis*) M
Tortula Moss (*Desmatodon plinthobius*) M

Riparian Corridor (exposed)

Channel and floodplain of the Pedernales River and open areas on terraces of the Pedernales River and lowermost Heinz Branch

Bald Cypress (*Taxodium distichum*) T
Eastern Sycamore (*Platanus occidentalis*) T
Black Willow (*Salix nigra*) T/S
Boxelder (*Acer negundo*) T
Rattlebush (*Sesbania drummondii*) S
Partridge Pea (*Chamaecrista fasciculata var. fasciculata*) H
Giant Spiderwort (*Tradescantia gigantea*) H
American Water-willow (*Justicia americana*) H
Controversial Weissia Moss (*Weissia controversa*) M

Slope (sheltered)

[canyon walls of Heinz Branch and sheltered areas on terraces of Pedernales River and lowermost Heinz Branch]

Shin Oak (*Quercus sinuata* var. *breviloba*) T/S
Cedar Elm (*Ulmus crassifolia*) T
Netleaf Hackberry (*Celtis laevigata* var. *reticulata*) T
Texas Oak (*Quercus buckleyi*) T
Carolina Basswood (*Tilia americana* var. *caroliniana*) T
Arizona Walnut (*Juglans major*) T
Escarpment Black Cherry [Wild Cherry] (*Prunus serotina* var. *eximia*) T/S
Gum Elastic [Bumelia] (*Sideroxylon lanuginosum* ssp. *lanuginosum*) T/S
Eve's Necklace (*Styphnolobium affine*) T/S
Wafer Ash [Common Hoptree] (*Ptelea trifoliata*) T/S
Mexican Buckeye (*Ungnadia speciosa*) S
Silktassel (*Garrya ovata* ssp. *lindheimeri*) S
Elbow Bush [Stretchberry] (*Forestiera pubescens*) S/V
Yaupon (*Ilex vomitoria*) S
Evergreen Sumac (*Rhus virens*) S
Texas Kidneywood [Beebush] (*Eysenhardtia texana*) S
Mustang Grape (*Vitis mustangensis*) V
Plateau Milkvine (*Matelea edwardsensis*) V
Pearl Milkweed Vine (*Matelea reticulata*) V
Saw Greenbriar [Catbriar] (*Smilax bona-nox*) V
Carolina Snailseed [Red-berried Moonseed] (*Cocculus carolinus*) V
Virginia Creeper (*Parthenocissus quinquefolia*) V
Poison Ivy [Climbing Poison Ivy] (*Toxicodendron radicans*) V
Scarlet Leatherflower (*Clematis texensis*) V
Alabama Supplejack (*Berchemia scandens*) V
Wand Butterfly-bush (*Buddleja racemosa*) H
Shrubby Boneset (*Ageratina havanensis*) H
Columbine (*Aquilegia canadensis*) H
Cedar Sage (*Salvia roemeriana*) H
Spanish Moss (*Tillandsia usneoides*) H
Mexican Flowering Fern (*Anemia mexicana*) F
Purple Cliffbrake (*Pellaea atropurpurea*) F
Alabama Lipfern (*Cheilanthes alabamensis*) F
Powdery Cloakfern (*Argyrochosma dealbata*) F

Little Ebony Spleenwort [Blackstem Spleenwort] (*Asplenium resiliens*) F
Seductive Entodon Moss (*Entodon seductrix*) M
Stereophyllum Moss (*Stereophyllum radiculosum*) M
Lichen (*Usnea* sp. cf. *U. cirrosa*, Sundew Beard Lichen) L
Lichen (*Candelaria* sp. cf. *C. concolor*, Candleflame Lichen) L

Riparian Corridor (sheltered)

Waterfall, channel, floodplain, and terrace of lower Heinz Branch

Bald Cypress (*Taxodium distichum*) T
Chinkapin Oak (*Quercus muehlenbergii*) T
Eastern Sycamore (*Platanus occidentalis*) T
American Elm (*Ulmus americana*) T
Arizona Walnut (*Juglans macrocarpa*) T
Pecan (*Carya illinoiensis*) T
Spicebush (*Lindera benzoin*) T/S
Redbay (*Persea borbonia*) T/S
Roughleaf Dogwood (*Cornus drummondii*) T/S
Rusty Blackhaw [Southern Blackhaw] (*Viburnum rufidulum*) T/S
Redbud (*Cercis canadensis* var. *texensis*) T/S
Mexican Plum (*Prunus mexicana*) T/S
Carolina Buckthorn (*Frangula caroliniana*) T/S
Red Mulberry (*Morus rubra*) T/S
Red Buckeye (*Aesculus pavia* var. *pavia*) S
Dwarf Palmetto [Texas Palmetto] (*Sabal minor*) S
American Beautyberry (*Callicarpa americana*) H/S
Turk's Cap (*Malvaviscus arboreus*) H/S
Green Dragon (*Arisaema dracontium*) H
Chatterbox Orchid [Giant Helleborine] (*Epipactis gigantea*) H
Great Plains Lady's Tresses (*Spiranthes magnicamporum*) H
Columbine (*Aquilegia canadensis*) H
Missouri Violet (*Viola missouriensis*) H
Yellow Passionflower (*Passiflora lutea*) H
Widow's Tears (*Commelina erecta*) H
Inland Sea Oats (*Chasmanthium latifolium*) G
Eastern Gamagrass (*Tripsacum dactyloides*) G
Horsetail (*Equisetum laevigatum*) F
Maidenhair Fern (*Adiantum capillus-veneris*) F

Lindheimer's Shieldfern (*Thelypteris ovata* var. *lindheimeri*) F
Amblystegium Moss (*Hygroamblystegium tenax* var. *tenax*) M
Didymodon Moss (*Didymodon tophaceus*) M
Eucladium Moss (*Eucladium verticillatum*) M
Bryoid Fissidens Moss (*Fissidens bryoides*) M

Columbine (*Aquilegia canadensis*) in flower. Illustration
by Nancy McGowan

APPENDIX B

Plants

A plant list for Westcave Preserve was begun in 1974 by John Ahrns, and he continued to add to it through 1981. An additional list was compiled by John Ahrns and David Lemke between 1981 and 1992, when the list was revised and printed as a brochure by Marshall C. Johnston, David Lemke, Margaret Campbell, John Gee, and John Ahrns. That list was revised in 2007. Additions were made during a BioBlitz in October 2010, when contributors included John Chenoweth, Laura Hansen, Nan Hampton, Bob Harms, Kirsti Harms, Sirpa Harms, and Terri Siegenthaler; during another BioBlitz on April 30, 2011, with the contributors being Michael Brewster, Chris Caran, Bill Carr, Paul Fushille, John Gerhart, Amber Ahrns Gosselin, Nan Hampton, Terri Siegenthaler, and Murray Walton; and during a survey of the Uplands by Bill Carr and Terri Siegenthaler on April 27, 2012. Nan Hampton compiled the 2007 plant list and in August 2015 reviewed the updated list for consistency with the USDA PLANTS Database. Scientific nomenclature is consistent with that of the USDA PLANTS Database (http://plants.usda.gov/java/).

Codes in Nativity Column

E = exotic, i.e., not native to Texas
N = native to Texas
N+ = endemic to Texas

Codes in Form Column

A = aquatic (submersed or submersed/emersed)
FA = annual forb
FAV = annual forb vine
FB = biennial forb
FP = perennial forb

FPV = perennial forb vine
GA = annual grass or grasslike plant;
GP = perennial grass or grasslike plant
PP = perennial fern or fern ally
S = shrub
T = tree
WV = woody vine

Family	Scientific Name	Common Name	Nativity	Form
Acanthaceae	Justicia americana	American Water-willow	N	FP
	Justicia pilosella	Tubetongue	N	FP
	Ruellia drummondiana	Drummond's Wild Petunia	N+	FP
	Ruellia humilis	Low Wild Petunia	N	FP
	Ruellia nudiflora	Wild Petunia	N	FP
Aceraceae	Acer negundo	Boxelder	N	T
Agavaceae	Dasylirion texanum	Texas Sotol	N	S
	Nolina texana	Sacahuista, Texas Beargrass	N	S
	Yucca constricta	Buckley Yucca	N	S
	Yucca rupicola	Twisted-leaf Yucca	N+	S
	Yucca treculeana	Spanish Dagger	N	S
Amaranthaceae	Amaranthus polygonoides	Tropical Amaranth	N	FA
Anacardiaceae	Rhus lanceolata	Prairie Flameleaf Sumac	N	S
	Rhus trilobata var. trilobata	Skunkbush Sumac	N	S
	Rhus virens	Evergreen Sumac	N	S
	Toxicodendron radicans	Climbing Poison Ivy	N	WV
	Toxicodendron radicans ssp. eximium	Shrubby Poison Ivy	N	S
Anemiaceae	Anemia mexicana	Mexican Flowering Fern	N	PP
Apiaceae	Chaerophyllum tainturieri	Wild Chervil, Hairyfruit Chervil	N	FA
	Conium maculatum	Poison Hemlock	E	FB
	Daucus pusillus	Southwestern Carrot	N	FA
	Hydrocotyle umbellata	Water Pennywort	N	FP
	Sanicula canadensis	Black Snakeroot	N	FP
	Spermolepis inermis	Smooth Scaleseed	N	FA
	Torilis arvensis	Beggarticks, Spreading Hedgeparsley	E	FA

Family	Scientific Name	Common Name	Nativity	Form
Aquifoliaceae	Ilex decidua	Deciduous Holly, Possumhaw	N	S
	Ilex vomitoria	Yaupon	N	S
Araceae	Arisaema dracontium	Green Dragon	N	FP
Arecaceae	Sabal minor	Dwarf Palmetto, Texas Palmetto	N	S
Asclepiadaceae	Asclepias asperula	Antelope Horns	N	FP
	Asclepias oenotheroides	Hierba de Zizotes	N	FP
	Asclepias tuberosa	Orange Milkweed, Butterfly Weed	N	FP
	Asclepias viridiflora	Wand Milkweed	N	FP
	Cynanchum barbigerum	Bearded Swallow-wort	N	FPV
	Funastrum crispum	Wavyleaf Milkweed Vine	N	FPV
	Funastrum cynanchoides	Twinevine	N	FP
	Matelea biflora	Purple Milkweed Vine	N	FP
	Matelea edwardsensis	Plateau Milkvine	N+	FPV
	Matelea gonocarpos	Milkweed Vine, Angularfruit Milkvine	N	FPV
	Matelea reticulata	Pearl Milkweed Vine	N	FPV
Aspleniaceae	Asplenium resiliens	Little Ebony Spleenwort, Blackstem Spleenwort	N	PP
Asteraceae	Achillea millefolium	Yarrow	E	FP
	Ageratina havanensis	Shrubby Boneset	N	S
	Amblyolepis setigera	Huisache Daisy	N	FA
	Ambrosia confertiflora	Weakleaf Bur Ragweed	N	FP
	Ambrosia psilostachya	Western Ragweed	N	FP
	Ambrosia trifida	Giant Ragweed	N	FA
	Amphiachyris dracunculoides	Broomweed	N	FA
	Aphanostephus riddellii	Riddell's Lazy Daisy	N	FP
	Baccharis neglecta	Poverty Weed, Roosevelt Weed	N	S
	Brickellia cylindracea	Brickellbush	N	FP
	Calyptocarpus vialis	Hierba del Caballo, Horseherb, Straggler Daisy	N	FP
	Carduus nutans	Nodding Thistle, Musk Thistle	E	FA, FB
	Centaurea melitensis	Maltese Star Thistle	E	FA
	Chaetopappa asteroides	Slender Bristletop, Arkansas Least Daisy	N	FA

Family	Scientific Name	Common Name	Nativity	Form
	Chaptalia texana	Silverpuff	N	FP
	Cirsium texanum	Texas Thistle	N	FP
	Conoclinium coelestinum	Blue Mistflower	N	FP
	Conyza canadensis	Horseweed	N	FA
	Coreopsis tinctoria	Goldenwave	N	FA
	Erigeron modestus	Plains Fleabane	N	FA
	Eupatorium havanense	Shrubby Boneset	N	S
	Eupatorium serotinum	Late Boneset	N	FP
	Evax prolifera	Flathead Rabbit Tobacco	N	FA
	Evax verna	Roundhead Rabbit Tobacco	N	FA
	Facelis retusa	Annual Trampweed	E	FA
	Gaillardia pulchella	Indian Blanket, Firewheel	N	FA
	Gaillardia suavis	Pincushion Daisy	N	FA
	Gamochaeta sp.	Cudweed	N	FA
	Grindelia lanceolata	Fall Gumweed	N	FP
	Grindelia squarrosa	Curlycup Gumweed	N	FA
	Gutierrezia texana	Texas Snakeweed	N	FA
	Helenium amarum	Yellow Sneezeweed	N	FA
	Helianthus maximiliani	Maximilian Sunflower	N	FP
	Heterotheca subaxillaris	Camphor Weed	N	FA
	Hymenopappus scabiosaeus var. corymbosus	Old Plainsman	N	FB
	Liatris punctata var. mucronata	Gayfeather	N	FP
	Lindheimera texana	Yellow Texas Star	N	FA
	Lygodesmia texana	Skeleton Plant	N	FP
	Melampodium leucanthum	Blackfoot Daisy	N	FP
	Packera obovata	Golden Groundsel, Roundleaf Ragwort	N	FP
	Palafoxia callosa	Palafoxia	N	FA
	Palafoxia rosea	Rosy Palafoxia	N	FA
	Pyrrhopappus pauciflorus	Texas False-dandelion	N	FP
	Ratibida columnifera	Mexican Hat	N	FP
	Rudbeckia hirta	Brown-eyed Susan	N	FP
	Solidago altissima	Tall Goldenrod	N	FP
	Solidago nemoralis	Gray Goldenrod, Prairie Goldenrod	N	FP
	Sonchus asper	Spiny Sow Thistle	E	FA

Family	Scientific Name	Common Name	Nativity	Form
	Sonchus oleraceus	Common Sow Thistle	E	FA
	Symphyotrichum divaricatum	Saltmarsh Aster	N	FP
	Symphyotrichum drummondii var. texanum	Texas Aster	N	FP
	Tetraneuris scaposa	Slender-stem Bitterweed	N	FP
	Thelesperma filifolium	Greenthread	N	FA
	Thelesperma simplicifolium	Navajo Tea	N	FP
	Thymophylla pentachaeta var. pentachaeta	Parralena, Fiveneedle Pricklyleaf, Dyssodia	N	FP
	Verbesina virginica	Frostweed	N	FP
	Vernonia lindheimeri	Woolly Ironweed	N	FP
	Viguiera dentata	Goldeneyes	N	FA
	Wedelia acapulcensis var. hispida	Hairy Wedelia, Zexmenia	N	FP
	Xanthium strumarium	Rough Cocklebur	N	FA
Berberidaceae	Mahonia swaseyi	Texas Barberry	N+	S
	Mahonia trifoliolata	Agarito, Agarita	N	S
Boraginaceae	Buglossoides arvensis	Corn Gromwell	E	FA
	Ehretia anacua	Anacua	N	T
	Heliotropium tenellum	White Heliotrope	N	FA
	Lithospermum incisum	Puccoon	N	FP
Brassicaceae	Arabis petiolaris	Rock Cress	N	FA
	Capsella bursa-pastoris	Shepherd's Purse	E	FA
	Draba cuneifolia	Whitlowgrass	N	FA
	Lepidium virginicum	Peppergrass	N	FA
	Lesquerella recurvata	Gaslight Bladderpod	N+	FA
	Nasturtium officinale	Watercress	E	FP
Bromeliaceae	Tillandsia recurvata	Ball Moss	N	FP
	Tillandsia usneoides	Spanish Moss	N	FP
Buddlejaceae	Buddleja racemosa	Wand Butterfly Bush	N+	S
Cactaceae	Coryphantha sulcata	Pineapple Cactus	N	S
	Cylindropuntia leptocaulis	Pencil Cactus, Tasajillo, Christmas Cactus	N	S
	Echinocactus texensis	Horsecrippler	N	S
	Echinocereus reichenbachii ssp. reichenbachii	Lace Cactus	N	S
	Echinocereus triglochidiatus	Claret Cup	N	S
	Escobaria missouriensis	Missouri Foxtail Cactus	N	S

Family	Scientific Name	Common Name	Nativity	Form
	Opuntia engelmannii var. lindheimeri	Lindheimer Prickly Pear, Texas Prickly Pear	N	S
	Opuntia macrorhiza	Common Prickly Pear	N	S
	Opuntia phaeacantha	Brownspine Prickly Pear	N	S
	Thelocactus setispinus	Hedgehog Cactus	N	S
Campanulaceae	Triodanis perfoliata	Clasping Venus' Looking Glass	N	FA
Caprifoliaceae	Lonicera albiflora	Western White Honeysuckle, Texas Honeysuckle	N	S
	Viburnum rufidulum	Southern Blackhaw, Rusty Blackhaw	N	S
Caryophyllaceae	Arenaria benthamii	Bentham Sandwort	N	FA
	Silene antirrhina	Sticky Catchfly	E	FA
	Stellaria prostrata	Prostrate Chickweed	N	FA
Cistaceae	Helianthemum rosmarinifolium	Rosemary Frostweed	N	FP
	Lechea sp.	Pinweed	N	FP
Commelinaceae	Commelina erecta	Widow's Tears	N	FP
	Tinantia anomala	False Dayflower	N	FA
	Tradescantia gigantea	Giant Spiderwort	N	FP
Convolvulaceae	Convolvulus equitans	Texas Bindweed	N	FPV
	Dichondra carolinensis	Ponyfoot	N	FP
	Dichondra recurvata	Tharp's Ponyfoot	N+	FP
	Evolvulus sericeus	White Evolvulus	N	FP
	Ipomoea lindheimeri	Lindheimer's Morning Glory	N	FPV
	Merremia dissecta	Alamo Vine	N	FPV
Cornaceae	Cornus drummondii	Roughleaf Dogwood	N	S
Crassulaceae	Sedum nuttallianum	Yellow Stonecrop	N	FA
Cucurbitaceae	Cucurbita foetidissima	Buffalo Gourd	N	FAV
	Ibervillea lindheimeri	Balsam Gourd	N	FPV
Cupressaceae	Juniperus ashei	Ashe Juniper	N	T/S
	Taxodium distichum	Bald Cypress	N	T
Cyperaceae	Carex amphibola	Band Sedge, Eastern Narrowleaf Sedge	N	GP
	Carex edwardsiana	Plateau Sedge	N+	GP
	Carex microdonta	Littletooth Sedge	N	GP
	Carex perdentata	Texas Meadow Sedge, Sand Sedge	N	GP

Family	Scientific Name	Common Name	Nativity	Form
	Carex planostachys	Cedar Sedge	N	GP
	Cyperus odoratus	Fragrant Flatsedge	N	GA
	Cyperus retroflexus	One-flower Flatsedge	N	GP
	Eleocharis sp.	Spike Sedge	N	GP
	Rhynchospora nivea	Whitetop Sedge, Showy Whitetop	N	GP
Ebenaceae	Diospyros texana	Mexican Persimmon, Texas Persimmon	N	S
Ephedraceae	Ephedra antisyphilitica	Mormon Tea, Clapweed	N	S
Equistaceae	Equisetum laevigatum	Horsetail	N	PP
Euphorbiaceae	Acalypha phleoides	Threeseed Mercury	N	FP
	Argythamnia humilis var. humilis	Low Silver Bush	N	FP
	Bernardia myricifolia	Oreja de Raton, Mouse Ears	N	S
	Chamaesyce angusta	Blackfoot Spurge	N	FP
	Chamaesyce fendleri	Fendler Spurge	N	FP
	Chamaesyce prostrata	Prostrate Sandmat	N	FA
	Chamaesyce villifera	Hairy Euphorbia, Hairy Sandmat	N	FA
	Cnidoscolus texanus	Texas Bull Nettle	N	FP
	Croton fruticulosus	Shrubby Croton, Bush Croton	N	S
	Croton monanthogynus	Prairie Tea	N	FA
	Croton texensis	Texas Croton	N	FA
	Euphorbia cyathophora	Wild Poinsettia	N	FA
	Euphorbia dentata	Dogtooth Spurge, Toothed Spurge	N	FA
	Euphorbia longicruris	Plateau Spurge, Wedgeleaf Spurge	N	FA
	Euphorbia marginata	Snow-on-the-Mountain	N	FA
	Euphorbia spathulata	Warty Spurge	N	FA
	Phyllanthus polygonoides	Knotweed Leafflower	N	FP
	Stillingia texana	Queen's Delight, Texas Toothleaf	N	FP
	Tragia brevispica	Shortspike Noseburn	N	FPV
	Tragia ramosa	Slender Noseburn	N	FP
Fabaceae	Acacia roemeriana	Catclaw	N	S
	Astragalus nuttallianus	Nuttall's Annual Milkvetch	N	FA

Family	Scientific Name	Common Name	Nativity	Form
	Cercis canadensis var. texensis	Redbud	N	T
	Chamaecrista fasciculata var. fasciculata	Partridge Pea	N	FA
	Dalea frutescens	Black Dalea	N	S
	Dalea nana	Dwarf Prairie Clover	N	FP
	Desmanthus acuminatus	Sharp-pod Bundleflower	N	FP
	Desmanthus velutinus	Velvet Bundleflower	N	FP
	Desmodium paniculatum	Panicled Tickclover, Panicled Trefoil	N	FP
	Desmodium psilophyllum	Simpleleaf Tick Trefoil, Sticktights	N	FP
	Eysenhardtia texana	Texas Kidneywood, Beebush	N	S
	Indigofera miniata	Scarlet Pea	N	FP
	Lespedeza texana	Texas Bushclover	N	FP
	Lupinus texensis	Bluebonnet	N	FA
	Medicago minima	Small Burclover, Burr Medick	E	FA
	Mimosa aculeaticarpa var. biuncifera	Catclaw Mimosa	N	S
	Mimosa borealis	Pink Mimosa	N	S
	Mimosa roemeriana	Sensitive Briar	N	FP
	Pediomelum latestipulatum var. appressum	Scurf Pea, Texas Plains Indian Breadroot	N+	FP
	Pediomelum rhombifolium	Brown-flowered Psoralea	N	FP
	Prosopis glandulosa	Honey Mesquite	N	T/S
	Rhynchosia senna var. texana	Snoutbean	N	FPV
	Senna lindheimeriana	Lindheimer's Senna, Velvetleaf Senna	N	FP
	Sesbania drummondii	Rattlebush	N	FP
	Sophora secundiflora	Texas Mountain Laurel	N	S
	Styphnolobium affine	Eve's Necklace	N	T
	Vicia ludoviciana	Deer Pea Vetch	N	FAV
Fagaceae	Quercus buckleyi	Texas Oak	N	T
	Quercus fusiformis	Scrub Live Oak	N	T
	Quercus muehlenbergii	Chinkapin Oak	N	T
	Quercus sinuata var. breviloba	Shin Oak	N	T/S
	Quercus stellata	Post Oak	N	T
Fumariaceae	Corydalis curvisiliqua	Scrambled Eggs	N	FA

Family	Scientific Name	Common Name	Nativity	Form
Garryaceae	*Garrya ovata ssp. lindheimeri*	Silktassel	N	S
Gentianaceae	*Centaurium beyrichii*	Mountain Pink	N	FA
	Centaurium texense	Lady Bird's Centaury	N	FA
	Eustoma exaltatum ssp. russellianum	Bluebell Gentian	N	FA
Geraniaceae	*Erodium cicutarium*	Redstem Stork's Bill	E	FA
	Erodium texanum	Stork's Bill	N	FA
	Geranium texanum	Texas Cranesbill, Texas Geranium	N	FA
Hippocastanaceae	*Aesculus pavia var. flavescens*	Yellow Buckeye	N	T
	Aesculus pavia var. pavia	Red Buckeye	N	T
Hydrangeaceae	*Philadelphus ernestii*	Canyon Mock Orange	N+	S
Hydrophyllaceae	*Nemophila phacelioides*	Baby Blue-eyes	N	FA
	Phacelia congesta	Blue Curls	N	FA
Iridaceae	*Nemastylis geminiflora*	Celestials	N	FP
	Sisyrinchium angustifolium	Blue-eyed Grass	N	FP
	Sisyrinchium chilense	Swordleaf Blue-eyed Grass	N	FP
Juglandaceae	*Carya illinoinensis*	Pecan	N	T
	Juglans major	Arizona Walnut	N	T
	Juglans microcarpa	Little Walnut	N	T/S
Juncaceae	*Juncus interior*	Inland Rush	N	GP
	Juncus marginatus	Common Rush, Grassleaf Rush	N	GP
Krameriaceae	*Krameria lanceolata*	Ratany	N	FP
Lamiaceae	*Hedeoma acinoides*	Annual Pennyroyal	N	FA
	Hedeoma drummondii	Mock Pennyroyal	N	FP
	Hedeoma reverchonii	False Pennyroyal	N	FP
	Lamium amplexicaule	Henbit, Deadnettle	E	FA
	Leonurus sibiricus	Motherwort, Honeyweed	E	FB
	Marrubium vulgare	Horehound	E	FP
	Monarda citriodora	Beebalm	N	FA
	Monarda punctata	Spotted Horsemint, Spotted Beebalm	N	FP
	Physostegia angustifolia	False Dragonhead	N	FP
	Salvia coccinea	Scarlet Sage	N	FA
	Salvia roemeriana	Cedar Sage	N	FP
	Salvia texana	Texas Sage	N	FP
	Scutellaria drummondii	Drummond Skullcap	N	FA

Family	Scientific Name	Common Name	Nativity	Form
	Scutellaria ovata	Heartleaf Skullcap	N	FP
	Scutellaria wrightii	Bushy Skullcap	N	FP
	Stachys crenata	Shade Betony, Mousesear	N	FA
	Teucrium canadense	American Germander	N	FP
	Warnockia scutellarioides	Brazos Mint	N	FA
Lauraceae	*Lindera benzoin*	Spicebush	N	S/T
	Persea borbonia	Redbay	N	S/T
Liliaceae	*Allium canadense var. fraseri*	Fraser's Upland Onion	N	FP
	Allium drummondii	Drummond's Wild-garlic	N	FP
	Cooperia drummondii	Rain Lily	N	FP
	Cooperia pedunculata	Broadleaf Rain Lily	N	FP
	Nothoscordum bivalve	Crow Poison	N	FP
	Zigadenus nuttallii	Death Camus	N	FP
Linaceae	*Linum hudsonioides*	Annual Flax	N	FA
	Linum rupestre	Rock Flax	N	FP
Loasaceae	*Mentzelia oligosperma*	Stick-leaf	N	FP
Malpighiaceae	*Galphimia angustifolia*	Thryallis	N	FP
Malvaceae	*Abutilon fruticosum*	Indian Mallow	N	FP
	Allowissadula holosericea	Velvetleaf Mallow	N	FP
	Callirhoe involucrata	Bracted Winecup	N	FP
	Malvaviscus arboreus	Turk's Cap, Wax Mallow	N	FP
	Pavonia lasiopetala	Rose Pavonia	N	S
	Rhynchosida physocalyx	Bladderpod Sida	N	FP
	Sida abutifolia	Creeping Sida, Spreading Fanpetals	N	FP
Meliaceae	*Melia azedarach*	Chinaberry	E	T
Menispermaceae	*Cocculus carolinus*	Red-berried Moonseed, Carolina Snailseed	N	FPV
Moraceae	*Ficus carica*	Common Fig, Edible Fig	E	S
	Maclura pomifera	Osage Orange, Horse Apple, Bois d'arc	N	T
	Morus microphylla	Texas Mulberry	N	T/S
	Morus rubra	Red Mulberry	N	T
Nyctaginaceae	*Boerhavia coccinea*	Scarlet Spiderling	N	FA
	Mirabilis albida	White Four O'clock	N	FP
	Mirabilis linearis	Linearleaf Four O'clock, Narrowleaf Four O'clock	N	FP

Family	Scientific Name	Common Name	Nativity	Form
	Mirabilis sp.	Wild Four O'clock, Marvel of Peru	E	FP
Oleaceae	Forestiera pubescens	Elbow Bush, Stretchberry	N	S
	Fraxinus albicans	Texas Ash	N	T
	Ligustrum japonicum	Japanese Privet	E	S
Onagraceae	Gaura brachycarpa	Shortfruit Gaura	N	FA
	Gaura suffulta	Lizard Tail, Bee Blossom	N	FA
	Oenothera macrocarpa ssp. marcocarpa	Fluttermill, Missouri Primrose	N	FP
	Oenothera speciosa	Showy Evening Primrose, Pinkladies	N	FP
	Oenothera triloba	Stemless Evening Primrose	N	FP
Orchidaceae	Corallorhiza wisteriana	Spring Coralroot	N	FP
	Epipactis gigantea	Giant Helleborine, Chatterbox Orchid	N	FP
	Spiranthes magnicamporum	Great Plains Lady's Tresses	N	FP
Oxalidaceae	Oxalis dillenii	Yellow Wood Sorrel	N	FP
	Oxalis drummondii	Violet Wood Sorrel, Drummond's Wood Sorrel	N	FP
Passifloraceae	Passiflora affinis	Bracted Passionflower	N	FPV
	Passiflora incarnata	Purple Passionflower	N	FPV
	Passiflora lutea	Yellow Passionflower	N	FPV
	Passiflora tenuiloba	Birdwing Passionflower	N	FPV
Phytolaccaceae	Phytolacca americana	Pokeweed	N	FP
	Rivina humilis	Pigeon Berry, Rougeplant	N	FP
Plantaginaceae	Plantago aristata	Bracted Plantain	N	FA
	Plantago helleri	Heller's Plantain	N	FA
	Plantago rhodosperma	Red-seeded Plaintain	N	FA
	Plantago wrightiana	Wright's Plantain, Tallow-weed	N	FA
Platanaceae	Platanus occidentalis	Eastern Sycamore	N	T
Poaceae	Aegilops cylindrica	Goatgrass	E	GA
	Andropogon glomeratus	Bushy Bluestem	N	GP
	Aristida oligantha	Oldfield Threeawn	N	GP
	Aristida purpurea var. longiseta	Longawn Threeawn	N	GP
	Aristida purpurea var. purpurea	Purple Threeawn	N	GP
	Bothriochloa ischaemum	King Ranch Bluestem	E	GP

Family	Scientific Name	Common Name	Nativity	Form
	Bothriochloa laguroides ssp. torreyana	Silver Bluestem	N	GP
	Bouteloua curtipendula	Sideoats Grama	N	GP
	Bouteloua dactyloides	Buffalo Grass	N	GP
	Bouteloua hirsuta	Hairy Grama	N	GP
	Bouteloua hirsuta var. pectinata	Tall Grama	N	GP
	Bouteloua rigidiseta	Texas Grama	N	GP
	Bouteloua trifida	Red Grama	N	GP
	Bromus lanceolata	Mediterranean Brome	E	GA
	Bromus pubescens	Chess, Hairy Woodland Brome	N	GP
	Cenchrus spinifex	Sandbur	N	GP
	Chasmanthium latifolium	Inland Sea Oats	N	GP
	Chloris cucullata	Hooded Windmill Grass	N	GP
	Chloris subdolichostachya	Shortspike Windmill Grass	N	GP
	Chloris verticillata	Windmillgrass	N	GP
	Cynodon dactylon	Bermudagrass	E	GP
	Dichanthelium acuminatum var. lindheimeri	Lindheimer Dichanthelium	N	GP
	Dichanthelium oligosanthes var. scribnerianum	Scribner's Dichanthelium, Heller's Rosette Grass	N	GP
	Dichanthium annulatum	Kleberg's Bluestem	E	GP
	Digitaria ciliaris	Crabgrass	N	GP
	Digitaria cognata	Fall Witchgrass	N	GP
	Elymus canadensis	Canada Wildrye	N	GP
	Elymus virginicus	Virginia Wildrye	N	GP
	Eragrostis barrelieri	Mediterranean Lovegrass	E	GA
	Eragrostis cilianensis	Stinkgrass	E	GA
	Eragrostis curtipedicellata	Gummy Lovegrass	N	GP
	Eragrostis intermedia	Plains Lovegrass	N	GP
	Eragrostis secundiflora	Red Lovegrass	N	GP
	Erioneuron pilosum	Hairy Tridens	N	GP
	Hilaria belangeri	Curly Mesquite	N	GP
	Leptochloa dubia	Green Sprangletop	N	GP
	Limnodea arkansana	Ozarkgrass	N	GA
	Melica nitens	Three-flower Melic	N	GP
	Muhlenbergia involuta	Canyon Muhly	N	GP

Family	Scientific Name	Common Name	Nativity	Form
	Muhlenbergia lindheimeri	Lindheimer Muhly	N	GP
	Muhlenbergia reverchonii	Seep Muhly	N	GP
	Muhlenbergia schreberi	Nimblewill	N	GP
	Muhlenbergia x involuta	Canyon Muhly	N	GP
	Nassella leucotricha	Texas Wintergrass, Speargrass	N	GP
	Oplismenus hirtellus	Basketgrass	N	GP
	Panicum anceps	Beaked Panicum	N	GP
	Panicum hallii	Hall's Panicum	N	GP
	Panicum obtusum	Vine Mesquite	N	GP
	Panicum rigidulum	Redtop Panicum	N	GP
	Panicum virgatum	Switchgrass	N	GP
	Paspalum distichum	Knotgrass	N	GP
	Paspalum pubiflorum	Hairyseed Paspalum	N	GP
	Poa annua	Annual Bluegrass	E	GA
	Schizachyrium scoparium	Little Bluestem	N	GP
	Setaria leucopila	Streambed Bristlegrass	N	GP
	Setaria reverchonii	Reverchon Bristlegrass	N	GP
	Setaria scheelei	Southwestern Bristlegrass	N	GP
	Sorghastrum nutans	Indiangrass	N	GP
	Sorghum halepense	Johnsongrass	E	GP
	Sporobolus clandestinus	Rough Dropseed	N	GP
	Sporobolus compositus var. drummondii	Meadow Dropseed	N	GP
	Sporobolus vaginiflorus	Poverty Dropseed	N	GA
	Tridens albescens	White Tridens	N	GP
	Tridens flavus	Purpletop	N	GP
	Tridens muticus	Slim Tridens	N	GP
	Tridens texanus	Texas Tridens, Texas Fluffgrass	N	GP
	Tripsacum dactyloides	Eastern Gamagrass	N	GP
	Vulpia octoflora	Six-weeks Fescue	N	GA
Polemoniaceae	Giliastrum incisum	Splitleaf Gilia	N	FP
	Giliastrum rigidulum	Blue Gilia	N	FP
	Phlox roemeriana	Yelloweye Phlox, Goldeneye Phlox	N+	FA
Polygalaceae	Polygala alba	White Milkwort	N	FP

Family	Scientific Name	Common Name	Nativity	Form
	Polygala lindheimeri	Lindheimer Milkwort, Purple Milkwort	N	FP
	Eriogonum annuum	Annual Wild Buckwheat	N	FA
	Rumex sp.	Dock	N	FA
Portulacaceae	*Phemeranthus aurantiacus*	Orange Flameflower, Orange Fameflower	N	FP
	Portulaca oleracea	Common Purslane	E	FA
	Portulaca pilosa	Chisme	N	FA
Primulaceae	*Samolus ebracteatus* ssp. *cuneatus*	Water Pimpernel, Limewater Brookweed	N	FA
	Samolus valerandi ssp. *parviflorus*	Thinleaf Water Pimpernel	N	FA
Pteridaceae	*Adiantum capillus-veneris*	Maidenhair Fern	N	PP
	Argyrochosma dealbata	Powdery Cloakfern	N	PP
	Astrolepis integerrima	Lipfern, Hybrid Cloakfern	N	PP
	Cheilanthes alabamensis	Alabama Lipfern	N	PP
	Cheilanthes horridula	Rough Lipfern	N	PP
	Pellaea atropurpurea	Purple Cliffbrake	N	PP
	Pellaea ovata	Cliffbrake, Ovateleaf Cliffbrake	N	PP
Ranunculaceae	*Anemone berlandieri*	Ten-petal Anemone	N	FP
	Anemone edwardsiana	Canyon Anemone	N+	FP
	Aquilegia canadensis	Columbine	N	FP
	Clematis drummondii	Old Man's Beard	N	FPV
	Clematis pitcheri	Purple Leatherflower	N	FPV
	Clematis texensis	Scarlet Leatherflower	N+	FPV
	Delphinium carolinianum	Prairie Larkspur, Carolina Larkspur	N	FP
Rhamnaceae	*Berchemia scandens*	Alabama Supplejack	N	WV
	Colubrina texensis	Snakewood, Texas Hog Plum	N	S
	Condalia hookeri	Brasil, Brazilwood	N	S
	Frangula caroliniana	Carolina Buckthorn	N	T/S
	Ziziphus obtusifolia	Lotebush	N	S
Rosaceae	*Geum canadense*	White Avens	N	FP
	Malus ioensis var. *texana*	Blanco Crabapple	N+	T/S
	Photinia serratifolia	Taiwanese Photinia	E	S
	Prunus mexicana	Mexican Plum	N	T

Family	Scientific Name	Common Name	Nativity	Form
	Prunus serotina var. eximia	Wild Cherry, Escarpment Black Cherry	N	T
	Rubus trivialis	Southern Dewberry	N	S
Rubiaceae	Cephalanthus occidentalis	Buttonbush	N	S
	Galium aparine	Catchweed Bedstraw	N	FA
	Galium circaezans	Woods Bedstraw, Licorice Bedstraw	N	FP
	Galium texense	Texas Bedstraw	N	FA
	Galium virgatum	Southwest Bedstraw	N	FA
	Stenaria nigricans var. nigricans	Bluets	N	FP
Rutaceae	Ptelea trifoliata	Wafer Ash, Common Hoptree	N	T
	Thamnosma texana	Dutchman's Breeches	N	FP
	Zanthoxylum hirsutum	Prickly Ash, Tickletongue, Toothache Tree	N	T/S
Salicaceae	Populus deltoides	Eastern Cottonwood	N	T
	Salix nigra	Black Willow	N	T
Sapindaceae	Sapindus saponaria var. drummondii	Western Soapberry	N	T
	Ungnadia speciosa	Mexican Buckeye	N	S
Sapotaceeae	Sideroxylon lanuginosum ssp. lanuginosum	Gum Elastic, Bumelia	N	T/S
Scrophulariaceae	Agalinis edwardsiana	Plateau Agalinis	N+	FA
	Agalinis heterophylla	Prairie Agalinis	N	FA
	Castilleja indivisa	Texas Paintbrush	N	FA
	Maurandella antirrhiniflora	Snapdragon Vine	N	FPV
	Mecardonia procumbens	Prostrate Mecardonia, Baby Jump-up	N	FP
	Penstemon cobaea	Foxglove	N	FP
	Verbascum thapsus	Common Mullein	E	FB
Smilacaceae	Smilax bona-nox	Catbriar, Saw Greenbriar	N	WV
	Smilax rotundifolia	Roundleaf Greenbriar	N	WV
	Smilax tamnoides	Hellfetter, Blackbristle Greenbriar	N	WV
Solanaceae	Chamaesaracha edwardsiana	Plateau False Nightshade, Edwards Plateau Five Eyes	N	FP
	Nicotiana repanda	Fiddleleaf Tobacco	N	FA
	Physalis cinerascens	Ground Cherry	N	FP

Family	Scientific Name	Common Name	Nativity	Form
	Solanum dimidiatum	Western Horsenettle	N	FP
	Solanum elaeagnifolium	Silverleaf Nightshade	N	FP
	Solanum ptycanthum	American Nightshade	N	FP
	Solanum rostratum	Buffalo Bur	N	FA
	Solanum triquetrum	Texas Nightshade	N	FP
Styracaceae	Styrax platanifolius	Sycamore-leaf Snowbell	N+	S
Thelypteridaceae	Thelypteris ovata var. lindheimeri	Lindheimer's Shieldfern	N	PP
Tiliaceae	Tilia americana var. caroliniana	Carolina Basswood	N	T
Ulmaceae	Celtis laevigata var. reticulata	Netleaf Hackberry	N	T
	Celtis laevigata var. texana	Texas Sugarberry	N	T
	Ulmus americana	American Elm	N	T
	Ulmus crassifolia	Cedar Elm	N	T
Urticaceae	Parietaria pensylvanica	Cucumber Pellitory, Pennsylvania Pellitory	N	FA
	Urtica chamaedryoides	Stinging Nettle, Heartleaf Nettle	N	FA
Verbenaceae	Aloysia gratissima	Whitebrush, Beebrush	N	S
	Callicarpa americana	American Beauty Bush, American Beautyberry	N	S
	Glandularia bipinnatifida var. bipinnatifida	Prairie Verbena	N	FP
	Glandularia pumila	Pink Vervain	N	FA
	Lantana urticoides	Texas Lantana	N	S
	Verbena canescens	Bracted Vervain	N	FP
	Verbena halei	Texas Vervain	N	FP
	Vitex agnus-castus	Common Chastetree	E	S
Violaceae	Hybanthus verticillatus	Nodding Green Violet	N	FP
	Viola missouriensis	Missouri Violet	N	FP
Viscaceae	Phoradendron tomentosum	Mistletoe	N	S
Vitaceae	Cissus trifoliata	Cow-itch Vine	N	WV
	Nekimias arborea	Peppervine	N	WV
	Parthenocissus heptaphylla	Sevenleaf Creeper	N+	WV
	Parthenocissus quinquefolia	Virginia Creeper	N	WV
	Vitis cinerea var. helleri	Spanish Grape	N	WV
	Vitis mustangensis	Mustang Grape	N	WV

APPENDIX C

Common Mosses

Bob Fulginiti

The following list of moss species is based on observations and collections at Westcave Preserve during two trips on February 5, 2008, and May 25, 2008.

Scientific nomenclature is consistent with that of the Integrated Taxonomic Information System (ITIS, http://www.itis.gov).

1. *Hygroamblystegium tenax* var. *tenax*
Common, on frequently to permanently wet limestone in and alongside Heinz Branch from the plunge pool to the Pedernales River. This species is frequently found growing intermingled with *Didymodon tophaceus* (see below), and although it is usually encrusted with limey secretions, it is the *Didymodon* that appears to be the active secretor.
US distribution: widespread

2. *Didymodon tophaceus*
Common, on wet, usually seeping limestone, especially dripping cliffs. Most abundant at the cave and plunge pool, but also found scattered along the creek bed to the river. This plant is known to be a tufa former.
US distribution: primarily western US, scattered in the east

3. *Entodon seductrix*
Infrequent, on bark at the base of hardwood trees and limestone boulders in the more mesic pockets on the canyon slopes.
US distribution: widespread in eastern North America to Texas

4. *Eucladium verticillatum*
Common, much the same as *Didymodon tophaceus*, that is, on wet limestone and tufa in drippy, seepy areas from the cave to the river, but more common

around the cave. This species is not known to be a tufa former.
US distribution: scattered across the US

5. *Fissidens bryoides*
Infrequent, on moist, shaded soil along the creek bed, with its abundance increasing downstream from the cave.
US distribution: widespread

6. *Leucodon julaceus*
Common, on Ashe Juniper bark especially a few feet above the soil, but occasionally on flat-topped limestone outcrops. This is one of the few mosses present on the preserve that uses Ashe Juniper bark as a substrate. Found along the dry upper reaches of the canyon slopes.
US distribution: eastern US

7. *Orthotrichum cupulatum*
Common, on the faces of large, dry limestone outcrops along the canyon walls and slopes.
US distribution: western and southwestern US

8. *Pleurochaete squarrosa*
On dry, limey soil in the open areas of the Ashe Juniper brakes in the Uplands part of the preserve.
US distribution: southeastern and southwestern US

9. *Sematophyllum adnatum*
Infrequent, on tree bark, occasionally even Ashe Junipers, in the Uplands canyon rim zone.
US distribution: eastern US to Texas

10. *Taxiphyllum taxiramuem*
Infrequent, within the creek bank on damp soil.
US distribution: eastern US, west to Texas, Arizona, and New Mexico

11. *Thelia hirtella*
Infrequent, on limestone outcrops along upper slopes of the canyon and on bark of hardwoods.
US distribution: eastern US to Texas

12. *Stereophyllum radiculosum*
Infrequent, on bark on trees along slopes of canyon.
US distribution: southern US

13. *Tortula plinthobia*
Common, on dry limestone outcrops along canyon walls.
US distribution: widespread

14. *Weissia controversa*
Common, in disturbed sites, frequently on exposed soil, creek bed, and
canyon slopes.
US distribution: widespread

15. *Weissia jamaicensis*
Common, on soil in the Uplands and along canyon slopes to the creek bed.
US distribution: southern and southwestern US

APPENDIX D

Invertebrates other than Butterflies

S. Christopher Caran and Nan Hampton compiled this list of the invertebrates (other than butterflies) of Westcave Preserve from personal observations and unpublished reports by unnamed staff members of the Lower Colorado River Authority (undated biological survey); William H. Russell and unnamed volunteers with the Texas Speleological Survey (undated cave survey); and Traci Ibarra and Erich Rose, Westcave Preserve staff members. This list represents the results of both limited systematic investigations and isolated observations. Although far from being a complete or even fully representative inventory of the invertebrates at Westcave Preserve, the list does constitute a basis for further research.

Scientific nomenclature is consistent with that of the Integrated Taxonomic Information System (ITIS, http://www.itis.gov). The validity of nomenclature marked with an asterisk (*) is not found on ITIS.

Phylum ANNELIDA, Segmented Worms

Class OLIGOCHAETA, Earthworms

Phylum ARTHROPODA, Jointed Invertebrates

Class ARACHNIDA

ORDER ARANEAE, SPIDERS

Family AGELENIDAE, Funnel Weavers
Barronopsis texana, Funnel Weaver

Family ARANEIDAE, Orb Weavers
Argiope aurantia, Yellow Garden Spider
Neoscona crucifera, Arboreal Orbweaver
Neoscona spp.

Family LINYPHIIDAE, Dwarf Weavers, Sheetweb Weavers
Frontinella communis, Bowl and Doily Weaver

Family LYCOSIDAE, Wolf Spiders
Pardosa sp., Thinlegged Wolf Spider

Family NEPHILIDAE
Nephila clavipes, Golden Silk Orbweaver

Family OXYOPIDAE, Lynx Spiders
Peucetia viridans, Green Lynx Spider

Family PISAURIDAE, Nursery Web Spiders
Dolomedes scriptus, Striped Fishing Spider

Family SCYTODES, Spitting Spiders
Scytodes sp., Spitting Spider

Family SICARIIDAE, Sixeyed Sicariid Spiders
Loxosceles reclusa, Brown Recluse

Family THERIDIIDAE, Cobweb Spiders
Latrodectus mactans, Southern Black Widow

Family TETRAGNATHIDAE, Longjawed Orbweavers
Tetragnatha sp., Longjawed Orbweaver

ORDER OPILIONES, DADDY LONGLEGS, HARVESTMEN
  Leiobunum sp., Harvestman

ORDER SCORPIONES, SCORPIONS
  *Family BUTHIDAE
  Centruoides vittatus, Striped Bark Spider

Class INSECTA, *Insects*
ORDER COLEOPTERA, BEETLES
  Family ELMIDAE, Riffle Beetles
  Hexacylloepus sp.

Microcylloepus sp.
Stenelmis sp.

Family LUTROCHIDAE, Travertine Beetles, Marsh-loving Beetles
Lutrochus sp.

ORDER DIPTERA, TRUE FLIES
Family CHIRONOMIDAE, Midges

Family TABANIDAE, Deer Flies, Horse Flies
Tabanus sp., Horse Fly

ORDER EPHEMEROPTERA, MAYFLIES
Family BAETIDAE, Small Minnow Mayflies
Camelobaetidius sp.
Baetis sp.

Family ISONYCHIIDAE, Brushlegged Mayflies
Isonychia sp.

Family LEPTOPHLEBIIDAE, Pronggills
Thraulodes sp.
Traverella sp.

Family LEPTOHYPHIDAE, Little Stout Crawlers
Leptohyphes sp.
Tricorythodes sp.

ORDER HEMIPTERA, TRUE BUGS
Family NAUCORIDAE, Creeping Water Bugs
Cryphocricos sp.

ORDER HYMENOPTERA, ANTS, BEES, WASPS
Family FORMICIDAE, Ants
Atta texana, Texas Leafcutting Ant
Pogonomyrmex barbatus, Red Harvester Ant

ORDER LEPIDOPTERA, MOTHS, BUTTERFLIES
Family EREBIDAE
Ascalapha odorata, Black Witch Moth

Family PRODOXIDAE, Yucca Moths
Tegeticula yuccasella, Yucca Moth

Family SATURNIIDAE, Giant Silkworm Moths, Royal Moths
Actias luna, Luna Moth
Antheraea polyphemus, Polyphemus Moth

Family SHINGIDAE, Hawk Moths, Hornworms, Sphinx Moths
Cocytius antaeus, Giant Sphinx Moth

ORDER MEGALOPTERA, ALDERFLIES, DOBSONFLIES, FISHFLIES
Family CORYDALIDAE, Dobsonflies, Fishflies, Helgrammites
Corydalus sp., Dobsonflies

ORDER ODONATA, DRAGONFLIES AND DAMSELFLIES
Family AESHNIDAE, Darners
Anax junius, Common Green Darner

Family COENAGRIONIDAE, Narrow Winged Damselflies, Pond Damsels
Argia sp., Dancers

Family LIBELLULIDAE, Common Skimmers, Skimmers
Plathemis lydia, Common Whitetail Dragonfly
Tramea lacerata, Black Saddlebags Dragonfly
Tramea onusta, Red Saddlebags Dragonfly

ORDER PLECOPTERA, STONEFLIES
Family PERLIDAE, Common Stoneflies
Anacroneuria sp.
Perlesta sp.

ORDER TRICHOPTERA, CADDISFLIES
Family HYDROPSYCHIDAE, Net-spinning Caddisflies
Cheumatopsyche sp.

Hydropsyche sp.
Smicridea sp.

Family PHILOPOTAMIDAE, Finger Net Caddisflies
Chimarra sp., Little Black Caddisflies

Family POLYCENTROPODIDAE, Trumpet Net Caddisflies
Polycentropus sp.

Class MALACOSTRACA
ORDER AMPHIPODA, AMPHIPODS
Family CRANGONYCTIDAE
Stygobromus russelli, Russell's Cave Amphipod

Phylum MOLLUSCA, Clams and Snails

Class BIVALVIA, *Bivalves, Clams*
ORDER HETERODONTA
Family CORBICULIDAE, Basket Clams
Corbicula fluminea, Asiatic Clam (exotic species)

Class GASTROPODA, *Snails*
ORDER BASOMMATOPHORA, FRESHWATER PULMONATES, POND SNAILS
Family PHYSIDAE, Bladder Snails
Physella sp.

ORDER STYLOMMATOPHORA, LAND SNAILS AND SLUGS
Family SPIRAXIDAE
Euglandina singleyana, Striate Wolfsnail

Family BULIMULIDAE
Rabdotus dealbatus, Whitewashed Rabdotus
Rabdotus mooreanus, Prairie Rabdotus

Phylum PLATYHELMINTHES, Flatworms

Class TREPAXONEMATA, *Planarians*

APPENDIX E

Butterflies

The main list of butterflies of Westcave Preserve was compiled by Dan Hardy in 2001–3. Species observed by Traci Ibarra and Erich Rose at the preserve were added in August 2015. The nomenclature was revised by Nan Hampton.

Scientific nomenclature is consistent with that of the Integrated Taxonomic Information System (ITIS, http://www.itis.gov).

Class INSECTA, Insects
ORDER LEPIDOPTERA, BUTTERFLIES AND MOTHS
Family PAPILIONIDAE, Swallowtail Butterflies
Battus philenor, Pipevine Swallowtail
Papilio cresphontes, Giant Swallowtail
Papilio glaucus, Eastern Tiger Swallowtail, Tiger Swallowtail
Papilio polyxenes, Black Swallowtail
Papilio troilus, Spicebush Swallowtail

Family PIERIDAE, Orange Tips, Whites, Sulphurs
Abaeis nicippe, Sleepy Orange
Anthocharis midea, Falcate Orangetip
Colias eurytheme, Orange Sulphur, Alfalfa
Kricogonia lyside, Lyside Sulphur
Nathalis iole, Dainty Sulphur
Phoebis sennae, Cloudless Sulphur
Pontia protodice, Checkered White
Pyrisitia lisa, Little Yellow, Little Sulphur
Zerene cesonia, Southern Dogface

Family LYCAENIDAE, Blues, Coppers, Hairstreaks, Gossamer-wing Butterflies
Atlides halesus, Giant Purple Hairstreak, Great Blue Hairstreak

Callophrys gryneus, Juniper Hairstreak
Callophrys henrici, Henry's Elfin
Calycopis isobeon, Dusky-Blue Groundstreak
Cupido comyntas, Eastern Tailed-Blue
Echinargus isola, Reakirt's Blue
Strymon melinus, Gray Hairstreak

Family NYMPHALIDAE, Admirals, Checker-spots, Fritillaries, Brushfooted Butterflies
  Agraulis vanillae, Gulf Fritillary
  Anaea andria, Goatweed Leafwing
  Anthanassa texana, Texan Crescent
  Asterocampa celtis, Hackberry Emperor
  Cercyonis pegala, Common Wood-Nymph
  Chlosyne lacinia, Bordered Patch
  Chlosyne nycteis, Silvery Checkerspot
  Chlosyne theona, Theona Checkerspot
  Danaus gilippus, Queen
  Danaus plexippus, Monarch
  Euptoieta claudia, Variegated Fritillary
  Heliconius charithonia, Zebra Heliconian
  Junonia coenia, Buckeye, Common Buckeye
  Libytheana carinenta, American Snout
  Megisto cymela, Little Wood Satyr
  Megisto rubricata, Red Satyr
  Mestra amymone, Common Mestra
  Nymphalis antiopa, Mourning Cloak
  Phyciodes graphica, Vesta Crescent, Graphic Crescent
  Phyciodes tharos, Pearl Crescent
  Polygonia interrogationis, Question Mark
  Vanessa atalanta, Red Admiral
  Vanessa cardui, Painted Lady
  Vanessa virginiensis, American Lady, American Painted Lady

Family HESPERIIDAE: Skippers
  Amblyscirtes celia, Celia's Roadside Skipper
  Atalopedes campestris, Sachem
  Copaeodes aurantiaca, Orange Skipperling
  Epargyreus clarus, Silverspotted Skipper

Erynnis funeralis, Funereal Duskywing
Erynnis horatius, Horace's Duskywing
Euphyes vestris, Dun Skipper
Hylephila phyleus, Fiery Skipper
Lerema accius, Clouded Skipper
Lerodea eufala, Eufala Skipper
Nastra julia, Julia's Skipper
Pyrgus communis, Common Checkered-Skipper
Pyrgus philetas, Desert Checkered-Skipper
Systasea pulverulenta, Texas Powdered-Skipper
Thorybes pylades, Northern Cloudywing
Urbanus proteus, Long-Tailed Skipper
Wallengrenia otho, Southern Broken-Dash

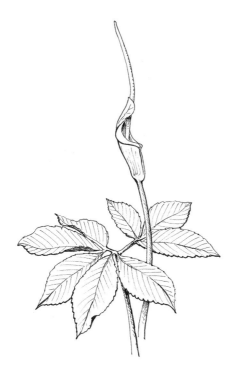

Green Dragon (*Arisaema dracontium*) in flower.
Illustration by Nancy McGowan

APPENDIX F

Fishes

S. Christopher Caran compiled this list (updated July 2015) of the fishes of Westcave Preserve from personal observations and unpublished records of unnamed investigators with the Lower Colorado River Authority and the Texas Parks and Wildlife Department. Additional observations were provided by John Ahrns and Steven Hubbell of Westcave Preserve.

There are many other species of fishes that might be found at the preserve, based on their known range and habitat preferences and the availability of suitable habitats within the preserve or the contiguous Pedernales River. Rather than speculate, the compiler has limited this list to those species known to be present based on identified specimens.

Scientific nomenclature is consistent with that of the Integrated Taxonomic Information System (ITIS, http://www.itis.gov).

Fishes known to be present in Heinz Branch are:

Superclass OSTEICHTHYES, Bony Fishes

Class ACTINOPTERYGII, Ray-finned Fishes
ORDER CYPRINIFORMES, MINNOWS, SUCKERS, CATFISHES, AND CHARACINS
    Family CYPRINIDAE, Minnows and Carps
    Campostoma anomalum, Central Stoneroller
    Carassius auratus, Goldfish (Introduced)
    Cyprinella lutrensis, Red Shiner
    Cyprinella venusta, Blacktail Shiner
    Notropis volucellus, Mimic Shiner

    Family CATOSTOMIDAE, Suckers
    Moxostoma congestum, Gray Redhorse

ORDER SILURIFORMES, SILURES, CATFISHES
    Family ICTALURIDAE, Bullhead Catfishes
    Ameiurus natalis, Yellow Bullhead

    Family POECILIIDAE, Livebearers
    Gambusia affinis, Western Mosquitofish

ORDER PERCIFORMES, BASSES, SUNFISHES, PERCHES, SCULPINS, AND CICHLIDS
    Family CENTRARCHIDAE, Sunfishes
    Lepomis cyanellus, Green Sunfish
    Lepomis macrochirus, Bluegill
    Lepomis megalotis, Longear Sunfish

    Family CICHLIDAE, Cichlids
    Herichthys cyanoguttatum, Rio Grande Cichlid (introduced; native to south-
       western Texas, but introduced into the Colorado River drainage)

Fishes of the Pedernales River at Hammetts Crossing (river reach adjacent to the mouth of Heinz Branch) are:

Superclass Class OSTEICHTHYES, Bony Fishes

Class ACTINOPTERYGII, Ray-finned Fishes
ORDER LEPISOSTEIFORMES, GARS
    Family LEPISOSTEIDAE, Gars
    Lepisosteus oculatus, Spotted Gar
    Lepisosteus osseus, Longnose Gar

ORDER CLUPEIFORMES, SALMONS, CHARS, TROUTS, WHITEFISHES, PIKES, MOON-
EYES, HERRINGS, SHAD, TARPONS, AND ANCHOVIES
    Family CLUPEIDAE, Herrings
    Dorosoma cepedianum, Gizzard Shad

ORDER CYPRINIFOMES, MINNOWS, SUCKERS, CATFISHES, AND CHARACINS
    Family CYPRINIDAE, Minnows and Carps
    Campostoma anomalum, Central Stoneroller
    Carassius auratus, Goldfish (introduced)
    Cyprinella lutrensis, Red Shiner
    Cyprinella venusta, Blacktail Shiner
    Cyprinus carpio, Common Carp
    Notropis volucellus, Mimic Shiner
    Pimephales vigilax, Bullhead Minnow

Family CATOSTOMIDAE, Suckers
Carpiodes carpio, River Carpsucker
Ictiobus bubalus, Smallmouth Buffalo
Moxostoma congestum, Gray Redhorse

ORDER SILURIFORMES, SILURES, CATFISHES
Family ICTALURIDAE, Bullhead Catfishes
Ictalurus punctatus, Channel Catfish
Pylodictis olivaris, Flathead Catfish

ORDER CYPRINODONTIFORMES, KILLIFISHES, PUPFISHES, AND LIVEBEARERS
Family POECILIIDAE, Livebearers
Gambusia affinis, Western Mosquitofish

ORDER PERCIFORMES, BASSES, SUNFISHES, PERCHES, SCULPINS, AND CICHLIDS
Family CENTRARCHIDAE, Sunfishes
Lepomis auritus, Redbreast Sunfish (introduced)
Lepomis cyanellus, Green Sunfish
Lepomis gulosus, Warmouth
Lepomis humilis, Orangespotted Sunfish
Lepomis macrochirus, Bluegill
Lepomis marginatus, Dollar Sunfish
Lepomis megalotis, Longear Sunfish
Lepomis microlophus, Redear Sunfish
Micropterus punctulatus, Spotted Bass (introduced; native to eastern Texas, but introduced into the Colorado River drainage)
Micropterus salmoides, Largemouth Bass
Micropterus treculii, Guadalupe Bass

Family PERCIDAE, Perches
Etheostoma spectabile, Orangethroat Darter
Percina carbonaria, Texas Logperch
Percina sciera, Dusky Darter

Family CICHLIDAE, Cichlids
Herichthys cyanoguttatum, Rio Grande Cichlid (introduced; native to southwestern Texas, but introduced into the Colorado River drainage)

APPENDIX G

Amphibians and Reptiles

John Ahrns, David Bennett, and S. Christopher Caran

This list was compiled from direct observations. There are many other species of amphibians and reptiles that might be found at Westcave Preserve, based on their known range and habitat preferences and the availability of suitable habitats within the preserve. The present list includes a few of the species, designated by a (P), that are very likely to be found there, although they were not observed. Rather than speculate further, the authors have limited the present list to those species either known or most likely to be present.

Scientific nomenclature is consistent with that of the Integrated Taxonomic Information System (ITIS, http://www.itis.gov).

Key:

P = Probable, but not confirmed by observation
I = Introduced (i.e., non-native species introduced to Texas that has spread into the preserve)

Class AMPHIBIA, Amphibians
ORDER ANURA, FROGS, TOADS
    Family SCAPHIOPODIDAE
    Scaphiopus couchii, Couch's Spadefoot (P)

    Family ELEUTHERODACTYLIDAE
    Eleutherodactylus marnockii, Cliff Chirping Frog

    Family HYLIDAE, Tree Frogs
    Acris blanchardi, Blanchard's Cricket Frog (P)
    Hyla chrysoscelis, Cope's Gray Treefrog

Hyla cinerea, Green Treefrog

Family BUFONIDAE, Toads
Anaxyrus woodhousii, Woodhouse's Toad

Family RANIDAE, Riparian Frogs, True Frogs
Lithobates berlandieri, Rio Grande Leopard Frog
Lithobates catesbeianus, American Bullfrog (P)
Lithobates sphenocephalus, Southern Leopard Frog (P)

Class REPTILIA, Reptiles
ORDER TESTUDINAES, TURTLES, TERRAPINS, TORTOISES
Family EMYDIDAE, Pond Turtles, Terrapins
Trachemys scripta elegans, Red-eared Slider
Terrapene ornata, Ornate Box Turtle (P)

Family TRIONYCHIDAE, Softshell Turtles
Apalone spinifera guadalupensis, Guadalupe Spiny Softshell

ORDER SQUAMATA, LIZARDS, SNAKES
Family GEKKONIDAE, Geckos
Hemidactylus turcicus, Mediterranean Gecko (I)

Family IGUANIDAE, American Arboreal Lizards, Iguanas
Anolis carolinensis, Green Anole
Crotaphytus collaris, Eastern Collared Lizard
Holbrookia lacerata lacerata, Plateau Earless Lizard
Phrynosoma cornutum, Texas Horned Lizard
Sceloporus olivaceus, Texas Spiny Lizard

Family SCINCIDAE, Skinks
Eumeces tetragrammus brevilineatus, Short-lined Skink

Family TEIIDAE, Ground Lizards, Racerunners
Cnemidophorus sexlineatus, Six-lined Racerunner

Family ANGUIDAE, Alligator Lizards
Gerrhonotus infernalis, Texas Alligator Lizard

Family COLUBRIDAE, Colubrids, Typical Snakes
Elaphe guttata emoryi, Great Plains Rat Snake
Elaphe obsoleta, Texas Rat Snake
Heterodon platirhinos, Eastern Hog-nosed Snake
Nerodia erythrogaster transversa, Blotched Water Snake
Pituophis catenifer sayi, Bullsnake (P)
Thamnophis marcianus, Checkered Garter Snake
Thamnophis proximus rubrilineatus, Redstripe Ribbon Snake

Family VIPERIDAE, Pit Vipers, Vipers
Agkistrodon contortrix laticinctus, Broad-banded Copperhead
Agkistrodon piscivorus leucostoma, Western Cottonmouth
Crotalus atrox, Western Diamondback Rattlesnake (P)
Crotalus molossus, Black-tailed Rattlesnake

Family ELAPIDAE, Cobras, Coral Snakes, Elapids, Kraits
Micrurus tener, Texas Coralsnake (P)

APPENDIX H

Birds

This list of birds is based on observations by John Gee and John Ahrns, "Birds of Westcave Preserve, Travis County, Texas," (revised 2007); Ed Faire, "Birds Seen in Westcave Preserve (as of June 22, 2013)"; Ron Martin, "Westcave Preserve new 40—2008 to 2012"; and many others and is supplemented with recent sightings of two additional species by Victor Emanuel and S. Christopher Caran. The scientific names, common names, and sequence of presentation follow the American Ornithologists' Union "AOU Checklist of North and Middle American Birds," 7th edition and supplements (http://www.americanornithology.org/content/aou-check-list-north-and-middle-american-birds-7th-edition-and-supplements). The common names of the families follow Jon L. Dunn and Jonathan Alderfer, *National Geographic Field Guide to the Birds of North America*, 5th ed. (2006). The Integrated Taxonomic Information System (ITIS) was also consulted regarding scientific names (http://www.itis.gov/).

The list was reviewed by Ethel Kutac and compiled by Nan Hampton.

Key:

I = Introduced into AOU area (i.e., the area covered by the AOU checklist)
N = Has not bred in AOU area, but occurs regularly as a non-breeding visitor

Class AVES, Birds
ORDER ANSERIFORMES, DUCKS, GEESE, SWANS, SCREAMERS, WATERFOWL
Family ANATIDAE, Ducks, Geese, and Swans
Anser albifrons, Greater White-fronted Goose
Chen caerulescens, Snow Goose
Branta canadensis, Canada Goose
Aix sponsa, Wood Duck

Anas discors, Blue-winged Teal
Anas crecca, Green-winged Teal

ORDER GALLIFORMES, FOWLS, GALLINACEOUS BIRDS
  Family ODONTOPHORIDAE, New World Quail
  Colinus virginianus, Northern Bobwhite

  Family PHASIANIDAE, Partridges, Grouse, Turkeys, Old World Quail
  Meleagris gallopavo, Wild Turkey

ORDER SULIFORMES, CORMORANTS
  Family PHALACROCORACIDAE, Cormorants
  Phalacrocorax auritus, Double-crested Cormorant

ORDER PELECANIFORMES, HERONS, PELICANS, IBIS
  Family PELECANIDAE, Pelicans
  Pelecanus erythrorhynchos, American White Pelican

  Family ARDEIDAE, Herons, Bitterns, allies
  Ixobrychus exilis, Least Bittern
  Ardea herodias, Great Blue Heron
  Ardea alba, Great Egret
  Bubulcus ibis, Cattle Egret
  Butorides virescens, Green Heron
  Nycticorax nycticorax, Black-crowned Night-heron

ORDER ACCIPITRIFORMES, HAWKS
  Family CATHARTIDAE, New World Vultures
  Coragyps atratus, Black Vulture
  Cathartes aura, Turkey Vulture

  Family ACCIPITRIDAE, Hawks, Kites, Eagles, allies
  Pandion haliaetus, Osprey
  Ictinia mississippiensis, Mississippi Kite
  Haliaeetus leucocephalus, Bald Eagle
  Circus cyaneus, Northern Harrier
  Accipter striatus, Sharp-shinned Hawk
  Accipter cooperii, Cooper's Hawk
  Buteo lineatus, Red-shouldered Hawk

Buteo platypterus, Broad-winged Hawk
Buteo swainsoni, Swainson's Hawk
Buteo albonotatus, Zone-tailed Hawk
Buteo jamaicensis, Red-tailed Hawk

ORDER GRUIFORMES, CRANES
Family GRUIDAE, Cranes
Grus canadensis, Sandhill Crane

ORDER CHARADRIIFORMES, ALCIDS, AUKS, GULLS, PLOVERS,
OYSTERCATCHERS, SHORE BIRDS
Family CHARADRIIDAE, Lapwings, Plovers
Charadrius vociferus, Killdeer

Family SCOLOPACIDAE, Sandpipers, Phalaropes, allies
Actitis hypoleucos, Common Sandpiper (N)
Bartramia longicauda, Upland Sandpiper
Scolopax minor, American Woodcock

Family LARIDAE, Gulls, Terns, Skimmers
Leucophaeus pipixcan, Franklin's Gull

ORDER COLUMBIFORMES, PIGEONS, DOVES
Family COLUMBIDAE, Pigeons, Doves
Columbina inca, Inca Dove
Columbina passerina, Common Ground Dove
Zenaida asiatica, White-winged Dove
Zenaida macroura, Mourning Dove

ORDER CUCULIFORMES, CUCKOOS
Family CUCULIDAE, Cuckoos, Roadrunners, Anis
Coccyzus americanus, Yellow-billed Cuckoo
Geococcyx californianus, Greater Roadrunner

ORDER STRIGIFORMES, OWLS
Family STRIGIDAE, Owls
Megascops asio, Eastern Screech-owl
Bubo virginianus, Great Horned Owl

ORDER CAPRIMULGIFORMES, GOATSUCKERS, NIGHTJARS, NIGHTHAWKS
Family CAPRIMULGIDAE, Goatsuckers
Chordeiles minor, Common Nighthawk
Phalaenoptilus nuttallii, Common Poorwill
Antrostomus carolinensis, Chuck-will's-widow
Caprimulgus vociferus, Whip-poor-will

ORDER APODIFORMES, HUMMINGBIRDS, SWIFTS
Family APODIDAE, Swifts
Chaetura pelagica, Chimney Swift

Family TROCHILIDAE, Hummingbirds
Archilochus colubris, Ruby-throated Hummingbird
Archilochus alexandri, Black-chinned Hummingbird

ORDER CORACIIFORMES, KINGFISHERS, ROLLERS
Family ALCEDINIDAE, Kingfishers
Megaceryle alcyon, Belted Kingfisher
Chloroceryle americana, Green Kingfisher

ORDER PICIFORMES, WOODPECKERS
Family PICIDAE, Woodpeckers, allies
Melanerpes aurifrons, Golden-fronted Woodpecker
Sphyrapicus varius, Yellow-bellied Sapsucker
Picoides scalaris, Ladder-backed Woodpecker
Picoides pubescens, Downy Woodpecker
Colaptes auratus, Northern Flicker

ORDER FALCONIFORMES, FALCONS
Family FALCONIDAE, Caracaras, Falcons
Caracara cheriway, Crested Caracara
Falco sparverius, American Kestrel

ORDER PASSERIFORMES, PERCHING BIRDS
Family TYRANNIDAE, Tyrant Flycatchers
Contopus cooperi, Olive-sided Flycatcher
Contopus virens, Eastern Wood-pewee
Empidonax virescens, Acadian Flycatcher

Empidonax alnorum, Alder Flycatcher
Empidonax minimus, Least Flycatcher
Empidonax spp.
Sayornis phoebe, Eastern Phoebe
Myiarchus cinerascens, Ash-throated Flycatcher
Myiarchus crinitus, Great Crested Flycatcher
Tyrannus verticalis, Western Kingbird
Tyrannus tyrannus, Eastern Kingbird
Tyrannus forficatus, Scissor-tailed Flycatcher

Family LANIIDAE, Shrikes
Lanius ludovicianus, Loggerhead Shrike

Family VIREONIDAE, Vireos
Vireo griseus, White-eyed Vireo
Vireo bellii, Bell's Vireo
Vireo flavifrons, Yellow-throated Vireo
Vireo solitarius, Blue-headed Vireo
Vireo gilvus, Warbling Vireo
Vireo olivaceus, Red-eyed Vireo

Family CORVIDAE, Crows, Jays
Cyanocitta cristata, Blue Jay
Aphelocoma californica, Western Scrub-jay
Corvus brachyrhynchos, American Crow
Corvus corax, Common Raven

Family HIRUNDINIDAE, Swallows
Progne subis, Purple Martin
Tachycineta bicolor, Tree Swallow
Petrochelidon pyrrhonota, Cliff Swallow
Hirundo rustica, Barn Swallow

Family PARIDAE, Chickadees, Titmice
Poecile carolinensis, Carolina Chickadee
Baeolophus bicolor, Tufted Titmouse
Baeolophus atricristatus, Black-crested Titmouse

Family AEGITHALIDAE, Long-tailed Tits, Bushtits
Psaltriparus minimus, Bushtit

Family CERTHIIDAE, Creepers
Certhia americana, Brown Creeper

Family TROGLODYTIDAE, Wrens
Salpinctes obsoletus, Rock Wren
Catherpes mexicanus, Canyon Wren
Thryothorus ludovicianus, Carolina Wren
Thryomanes bewickii, Bewick's Wren
Troglodytes aedon, House Wren
Troglodytes hiemalis, Winter Wren

Family REGULIDAE, Kinglet
Regulus satrapa, Golden-crowned Kinglet
Regulus calendula, Ruby-crowned Kinglet

Family SILVIIDAE, Old World Warblers, Gnatcatchers
Polioptila caerulea, Blue-gray Gnatcatcher

Family TURDIDAE, Thrushes
Sialia sialis, Eastern Bluebird
Catharus ustulatus, Swainson's Thrush
Catharus guttatus, Hermit Thrush
Turdus migratorius, American Robin

Family MIMIDAE, Mockingbirds, Thrashers
Mimus polyglottos, Northern Mockingbird

Family STURNIDAE, Starlings
Sturnus vulgaris, European Starling (I)

Family BOMBYCILLIDAE, Waxwings
Bombycilla cedrorum, Cedar Waxwing

Family PARULIDAE, Wood-warblers
Parkesia motacilla, Louisiana Waterthrush

Mniotilta varia, Black-and-white Warbler
Oreothlypis celata, Orange-crowned Warbler
Oreothlypis ruficapilla, Nashville Warbler
Geothlypis philadelphia, Mourning Warbler
Geothlypis trichas, Common Yellowthroat
Setophaga americana, Northern Parula
Setophaga magnolia, Magnolia Warbler
Setophaga petechia, Yellow Warbler
Setophaga coronata, Yellow-rumped Warbler
Setophaga dominica, Yellow-throated Warbler
Setophaga virens, Black-throated Green Warbler
Setophaga chrysoparia, Golden-cheeked Warbler
Basileuterus rufifrons, Rufous-capped Warbler
Cardellina pusilla, Wilson's Warbler
Icteria virens, Yellow-breasted Chat

Family EMBERIZIDAE, Emberizids
Melozone fuscus, Canyon Towhee
Pipilo maculatus, Spotted Towhee
Pipilo erythrophthalmus, Eastern Towhee
Aimophila ruficeps, Rufous-crowned Sparrow
Peucaea cassinii, Cassin's Sparrow
Spizella passerina, Chipping Sparrow
Spizella pallida, Clay-colored Sparrow
Spizella pusilla, Field Sparrow
Pooecetes gramineus, Vesper Sparrow
Chondestes grammacus, Lark Sparrow
Passerculus sandwichensis, Savannah Sparrow
Ammodramus savannarum, Grasshopper Sparrow
Ammodramus leconteii, Le Conte's Sparrow
Passerella iliaca, Fox Sparrow
Melospiza melodia, Song Sparrow
Melospiza lincolnii, Lincoln's Sparrow
Zonotrichia albicollis, White-throated Sparrow
Zonotrichia querula, Harris's Sparrow
Zonotrichia leucophrys, White-crowned Sparrow
Junco hyemalis, Dark-eyed Junco

Family CARDINALIDAE, Cardinals, Saltators, allies
Piranga rubra, Summer Tanager
Cardinalis cardinalis, Northern Cardinal
Pheucticus ludovicianus, Rose-breasted Grosbeak
Passerina caerulea, Blue Grosbeak
Passerina cyanea, Indigo Bunting
Passerina ciris, Painted Bunting
Spiza americana, Dickcissel

Family ICTERIDAE, Blackbirds
Agelaius phoeniceus, Red-winged Blackbird
Sturnella magna, Eastern Meadowlark
Sturnella neglecta, Western Meadowlark
Quiscalus quiscula, Common Grackle
Molothrus ater, Brown-headed Cowbird
Icterus spurius, Orchard Oriole
Icterus galbula, Baltimore Oriole

Family FRINGILLIDAE, Fringilline and Cardueline Finches
Haemorhous purpureus, Purple Finch
Haemorhous mexicanus, House Finch
Spinus pinus, Pine Siskin
Spinus psaltria, Lesser Goldfinch
Spinus tristis, American Goldfinch

Family PASSERIDAE, Old World Sparrows
Passer domesticus, House Sparrow (I)

APPENDIX I

Mammals

John Ahrns, David Bennett, Melissa Meierhofer, Leah M. Miller, and S. Christopher Caran

This list was compiled from direct observations. There are many other species of mammals that might be found at Westcave Preserve, based on their known range and habitat preferences and the availability of suitable habitats within the preserve. The present list includes a few of the species, designated by a (P), that are very likely to be found there, although they were not observed. Rather than speculate further, the authors have limited the present list to those species either known or most likely to be present.

Scientific nomenclature is consistent with that of the Integrated Taxonomic Information System (ITIS, http://www.itis.gov).

Key:

P = Probable, but not confirmed by observation
H = Historic (formerly extant)
I = Introduced (i.e., non-native species that was introduced to Texas and has spread into the preserve)

Class MAMMALIA, Mammals
ORDER DIDELPHIMORPHA, OPOSSUMS
　　Family DIDELPHIDAE, Opossums
　　Didelphis virginiana, Virginia Opossum

ORDER SORICOMORPHA, SHREWS AND MOLES
　　Family SORICIDAE, Shrews
　　Cryptotis parva, Least Shrew (P)

ORDER CHIROPTERA, BATS
Family VESPERTILIONIDAE, Vespertilionid Bats
Myotis velifer, Cave Myotis
Lasiurus borealis, Eastern Red Bat (P)
Perimyotis subflavus, Tri-colored Bat

Family MOLOSSIDAE, Free-tailed Bats
Tadarida brasiliensis mexicana, Mexican Free-tailed Bat

ORDER CINGULATA, ARMADILLOS
Family DASYPODIDAE, Armadillos
Dasypus novemcinctus, Nine-banded Armadillo

ORDER LAGOMORPHA, LAGOMORPHS
Family LEPORIDAE, Rabbits and Hares
Sylvilagus floridanus, Eastern Cottontail
Lepus californicus, Black-tailed Jackrabbit

ORDER RODENTIA, RODENTS
Family SCIURIDAE, Squirrels, Marmots, Chipmunks
Otospermophilus variegatus, Rock Squirrel
Sciurus niger, Eastern Fox Squirrel

Family HETEROMYIDAE, Kangaroo Mice, Kangaroo Rat, Pocket Mice
Perognathus merriami, Merriam's Pocket Mouse (P)
Chaetodipus hispidus, Hispid Pocket Mouse (P)

Family CASTORIDAE, Beavers
Castor canadensis, American Beaver (P or H)

Family ERETHIZONTIDAE, New World Porcupines
Erethizon dorsatus, North American Porcupine

Family MYOCASTORIDAE, Nutrias
Myocastor coypus, Nutria (I)

ORDER CARNIVORA, CARNIVORES
Family CANIDAE, Canids
Canis latrans, Coyote

Urocyon cinereoargenteus, Common Gray Fox

Family PROCYONIDAE, Procyonids
Bassariscus astutus, Ringtail
Procyon lotor, Common Raccoon

Family MEPHITIDAE, Skunks
Mephitis mephitis, Striped Skunk
Conepatus leuconotus, Hog-nosed Skunk

Family FELIDAE, Cats
Puma concolor, Mountain Lion (P or H)
Lynx rufus, Bobcat (P)

ORDER ARTIODACTYLA, EVEN-TOED UNGULATES
Family CERVIDAE, Cervids
Odocoileus virginianus, White-tailed Deer

Family SUIDAE, Hogs, Pigs
Sus scrofa, Pig (feral), Wild Boar (I)

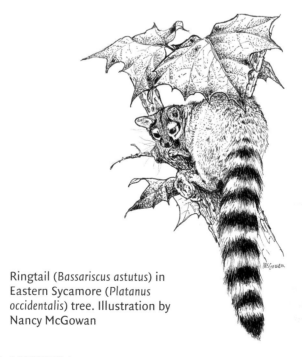

Ringtail (*Bassariscus astutus*) in
Eastern Sycamore (*Platanus
occidentalis*) tree. Illustration by
Nancy McGowan

SELECTED REFERENCES

There are many excellent sources of information about the natural and human history of the central Texas area, including Westcave Preserve. Below are some of the most useful and accessible field guides and other references. Some of these works may be out of print, but most can be found in larger libraries. Other data sources can be accessed online.

Human History, Outdoor Education, and Educational Facilities

Good, A. H. 1938. *Park and Recreation Structures.* Washington, DC: United States Department of the Interior, National Park Service, variously paginated.

Heilbron, J. L. 1999. *The Sun in the Church: Cathedrals as Solar Observatories.* Cambridge, MA: Harvard University Press, 384 pp.

Krutch, J. W. 2010. *The Desert Year.* Iowa City: University of Iowa Press, 271 pp.

Louv, Richard. 2006. *Last Child in the Woods: Saving Our Children from Nature-deficit Disorder.* Chapel Hill, NC: Algonquin Books, 335 pp.

McGuire, James Patrick. 1983. *Hermann Lungkwitz: Romantic Landscapist on the Texas Frontier.* Austin: University of Texas Press, 240 pp.

Olmsted, Frederick Law. 1857 (reprinted 1978). *A Journey through Texas: Or a Saddle-trip on the Southwestern Frontier.* Austin: University of Texas Press, 516 pp.

Sweet, Alexander Edwin. 1986. *Alex Sweet's Texas: The Lighter Side of Texas History.* Austin: University of Texas Press, 202 pp.

Turner, E. S.; T. R. Hester; and R. L. McReynolds. 2011. *Stone Artifacts of Texas Indians,* 3rd ed. Lanham, MD: Taylor Trade Publishing, 400 pp.

Natural History

Abbott, J. C. 2005. *Dragonflies and Damselflies of Texas and the South-central United States: Texas, Louisiana, Arkansas, Oklahoma, and New Mexico.* Princeton, NJ: Princeton University Press, 344 pp.

Bedichek, Roy. 1947 (reprinted 1975). *Adventures with a Texas Naturalist.* Austin: University of Texas Press, 368 pp.

Brune, Gunnar. 1981 (reprinted 2002). *Springs of Texas.* Fort Worth: Branch-Smith, Inc.; reprint, College Station: Texas A&M University Press, 566 pp.

Correll, D. S., and M. C. Johnston. 1970 (and subsequent addenda and errata). *Manual of the Vascular Plants of Texas.* Renner: Texas Research Foundation, 1,881 pp.

Crum, H. A., and L. E. Anderson. 1981. *Mosses of Eastern North America*, 2 vols. New York: Columbia University Press, 1,328 pp.

Davis, W. B., and D. J. Schmidly. 1994. *The Mammals of Texas*. Austin: Texas Parks and Wildlife Department, 338 pp.

Dixon, J. R. 2000. *Amphibians and Reptiles of Texas*. College Station: Texas A&M University Press, 421 pp.

Enquist, Marshall. 1987. *Wildflowers of the Texas Hill Country*. Austin, TX: Lone Star Botanical, 275 pp.

Finsley, Charles. 1999. *A Field Guide to Fossils of Texas*. Houston, TX: Gulf Publishing Company, 224 pp.

Hill, Robert T. 1901. *Geography and Geology of the Black and Grand Prairies with Detailed Descriptions of the Cretaceous Formations and Special Reference to Artesian Waters*. Washington, DC: Government Printing Office, 666 pp.

Kyle, Paul D. 2005. *Chimney Swift Towers: New Habitat for America's Mysterious Birds—A Construction Guide*. College Station: Texas A&M University Press, 96 pp.

———, and G. Z. Kyle. 2005. *Chimney Swifts, America's Mysterious Birds above the Fireplace*. College Station: Texas A&M University Press, 152 pp.

Larkin, T. J., and G. W. Bomar. 1983. *Climatic Atlas of Texas*. Austin: Texas Department of Water Resources, LP-192, 147 pp.

Lynch, Brother David. 1981. *Native and Naturalized Woody Plants of Austin and the Hill Country*. Austin, TX: St. Edward's University, 180 pp.

Neck, R. W. 1996. *A Field Guide to Butterflies of Texas*. Houston, TX: Gulf Publishing Company, 323 pp.

Reese, W. D. 1984. *Mosses of the Gulf South*. Baton Rouge: Louisiana State University Press, 252 pp.

Sibley, D. A. 2000. *The Sibley Guide to Birds*. New York: Alfred A. Knopf, 544 pp.

Spearing, Darwin. 1991. *Roadside Geology of Texas*. Missoula, MT: Mountain Press Publishing Company, 418 pp.

Storer, John H. 1953. *The Web of Life: A First Book of Ecology*. New York: Devin-Adair Publishing Company, 122 pp.

Thomas, Charles; T. H. Bonner; and B. G. Whiteside. 2007. *Freshwater Fishes of Texas*. College Station: Texas A&M University Press, 202 pp.

Wrede, Jan. 2005. *Trees, Shrubs, and Vines of the Texas Hill Country*. College Station: Texas A&M University Press, 246 pp.

Lindheimer prickly pear (*Opuntia engelmannii* var. *lindheimeri*) in flower. Illustration by Nancy McGowan

INDEX